GrowthTime!

A COACHING FABLE

THE CLEAR PATH TO UNLOCK YOUR BEST LIFE & LEADERSHIP

QUINN "COACH Q" HARWOOD

First published in 2025
© 2025 by Quinn Harwood
GrowthTime! The Clear Path to Unlock Your Best Life & Leadership,
Quinn Harwood

ISBN Paperback [979-8-9924557-1-7]
ISBN Hardback [979-8-9924557-0-0]

Created in conjunction with The Book Shelf Ltd:
Editor: Shelby Jones
Typesetter: Kyle Albuquerque
Cover designer: Niall Burgess
Proofreader: Gemma Rowlands

www.coachqharwood.com

DEDICATION

"To all those next generation leaders, mid–level managers and aspiring professionals hungry to win in life and leadership... GrowthTime! is for you!"

TABLE OF CONTENTS

Part 2 – Leadership

THE GROWTH JOURNEY BEGINS

To the Next Generation of Leaders,

I have heard your cry — the internal restless plea of confusion, self-doubt, and uncertainty — one hungering for significance and success. I know you crave freedom and the opportunity to impact this world.

Just as I did.

By now, you are fully acquainted with the tempest raging within and external pressures sabotaging your peace, stealing your confidence, and threatening your future. So far, you have undoubtedly encountered obstacles, roadblocks, and debris warring against your soul and mission. You probably aren't surprised to find yourself stuck in your headspace, questioning your skills in life and leadership.

*So, who and what are the villains in your story? You may have encountered those who don't **care** about you and others unwilling to **commit** to your career growth. Life will also put counterfeit leaders who you do not **trust** in your journey or bring bad intentions, hindering the fulfillment of your God-given purpose.*

In your quest, you charge down what I call the "unclear path," searching for the road to personal growth and development. So far, reading, scrolling social media, listening to podcasts, taking a personality test, or joining groups have all been part of your journey.

Yet, without mastering the fundamentals of life and leadership, you cannot go further, faster, or achieve fulfillment. **GrowthTime!** presents a clear path.

The truth is you were created to be a great 21st-century leader – one full of vision who wants to break through self-limiting beliefs and impact an increasingly bleak and disconnected world.

You will need to be strong in life and leadership.

GrowthTime! is a personal growth and development journey unlocking and unleashing your best life and leadership. It will transform, elevate, and empower you to deliver the desired results in the workplace and at home.

This book serves as a weapon to win the war and silence a desperate cry. It is a life coaching journey that follows our protagonist, Peter, venturing from an unsettled aspiring professional athlete to a business leader on a quest to find himself, purpose, and achieve his potential.

On his travels, Peter meets the mysterious Coach G, the head coach of Max-Potential Academy. He makes a bold offer forever changing Peter's life trajectory. Winding through different villages, towns, and cities, he is forced to face fundamental growth lessons that he will need to master.

Join him with the support of Coach G and team MPA, who clarify Peter's identity and purpose. Understand how Peter is empowered to recognize allies and enemies, overcome his limiting belief system, and create game-changing habits to free himself from the hypocrite monster within.

As Peter embraces challenging truths and forms a blossoming relationship with Coach G, a new version of himself emerges. With aversions and unexpected lifestyle changes, Peter's focus shifts to graduating MPA and mastering the core growth lessons of leadership. He learns, as you will, to master foundational leadership principles, establish winning mindsets, and develop coaching plays for his peeps to be a great 21st-century leader.

Be confident. This GrowthTime! path was forged in the fires of my own personal and leadership experiences. Whether you are facing self-inflicted challenges, a health crisis, financial adversity, a broken relationship, leadership pains or professional failure, you will learn how to rise above and find significance and success.

My greatest joy has been coaching thousands of life-changing sessions with leaders like you. These leaders silenced the self-sabotaging cry and allowed the hunger for success to consume.

Seeing my coachees win at life and in leadership has fulfilled my heart's cry.

Now it's your time. Your time for GrowthTime! You are invited to take this journey with Peter. There are questions and exercises to guide your growth at the end of each section.

Be strong and bold, for the Great Growth Coach – God himself – is watching over your growth journey.

It is time to change the world you influence,

Coach Q

THE POWER OF U!

Fire out of
the Gate!

Peter ducked into his Chevy Camaro, his long frame squashed against brown moving boxes. Everything he owned was jammed in that tiny, two-door T-top. After adjusting his navigation system, he glanced at his favorite basketball poking out of a box on the passenger seat before pushing the aux in.

"You only get one shot, do not miss your chance to blow, this opportunity comes once in a lifetime..."[1] Peter bopped his head, rapping hard, as he shoved his foot on the accelerator. The booming bass drowned the screech of his tires as he scorched rubber down his parents' driveway.

"Smoke 'em," he seethed. He clenched the steering wheel, burning with the frustrations and pain of his youth. Chips scattered the street. Peter looked ahead – to the future. He rolled his shoulders, stuck his chin up, and peeled for it.

It was the perfect fall afternoon to break for his new life.

The rollercoaster ride through his troubled teens was over with his college degree in tow. The last thing on his mind was standing before the juvenile judge again, awaiting a 12-month probation sentence and a stint of community service. Adulting was fixed on the horizon of Interstate 81, due west.

As the lyrics blared fame, a name, and fortune, a dream he had dreamt came to him. But, his first shot had been an airball.

"His palms are sweaty, knees weak, arms are heavy... mom's spaghetti," Peter thrummed, recalling his sweat-soaked hours on the basketball court, endless nights shooting jump shots at the Brokin' Rim hoops park, grinding the weights, firing through speed and agility camps.

He had transformed from a short, unathletic kid to playing college basketball for the Ivy Cats, an unknown school buried in the Deep South. From the knee-bouncing, nail-biting kid on the bench to cracking the starting line-up in his senior year, Peter made strides despite his inner demons screeching that he was unworthy and undeserving.

His senior year was his one shot to blow... and he did. Leading his team to unprecedented heights and a championship year. When the League came looking for him, he knew his star was rising.

The League was the epitome of success. It was where the global top 400 basketball players were separated into teams, gathering every year for nine months to compete for a championship — anyone who was anyone dreamed of making it there. The athletes received all the praise, recognition, and perks of being a celebrity... shooting life's hoops on a pedestal above the rest.

Peter was confident this would declare his arrival into adulthood and confirm his standing in the world. His significance would be locked in. The problem was he doubted he had what it took.

Despite the bravado self-talk and the music-infused hype train, Peter couldn't shake the thoughts from his first tryout with the League. Overwhelmed and outmatched by the elite competition, he wilted under expectations.

A complete airball.

Disappointment bombs blew his foundation. He was sent home packing just days into the event. The explosion revealed that the stage was too bright and his mask of confidence too thin to sustain the impact. No matter how much he tried, he couldn't quiet the coach's voice: "Peter, the League isn't for everyone."

It fed into his insecurities and caused a month-long shutdown. Was his dream really over? Peter shut his bedroom door, closed the curtains, and ate crumbs throughout the day. He gnawed his fingernails raw, thinking of who and what he was now.

As he battled his spiraling emotional descent, Peter received an unexpected call from the director of the Bluff Speedsters. The Speedsters were part of the Midwest Farmland League (MFL). The MFL was a cluster of pro-basketball teams from farmland cities filled with League hopefuls such as himself, people trying to prove they belonged... and clinging to the hope of another shot at glory.

The call gave Peter renewed hope. He dragged himself from his isolated pit, opened the curtains, and chowed down a full meal for the first time in weeks.

The MFL was far from glory. It was a minor league possessing a unique subculture, but Peter wasn't ready to throw in the towel. So, he packed all his belongings, including his leather worn basketball, and headed out. It was an injection of fresh fuel, and he burned octane on his drive to the Midwest.

Peter raced towards the Bluffs, a town on the barren plains of no-man's land. It lacked the luster of the League and didn't match the idealist vision Peter had created, but it was a fresh start.

A sliver of hope.

Peter's hand clenched the wheel as his thoughts wandered about how he got here. If he were honest, pain had been his motivator. He could still hear the creak of the garage door opening in the late evening, followed by the *thud, thud, thud* of his father's footsteps. The unease of him beelining for the family room wet bar, listening to the *clack* of ice cubes dropping into a whiskey glass... holding his breath for what would come.

Tiptoe. Stay low.

Beads of sweat ran down Peter's face at the memory. He pressed the gas pedal to swerve past the sedan going 80mph in the left lane.

A sequestered storm was unfurling.

Peter chewed his lip and winced to feel the stitch marks. Even thinking of Dad's anger was enough to disturb him. Nothing ever pleased the man. His older brother, bent on hurling his pent-up hostility on Peter, rivalled that. Their combative fire burned through their teenage years. Peter glanced in the rearview mirror, catching sight of the scar, a constant reminder of the underlying enmity.

Yeah, the heroes of his life had betrayed him, and the safety of seclusion or quick-witted insults were his weapons. He had no clue about the toxicity of resentment webbing his heart.

Peter eased his grip on the wheel. The chaos was behind him. Wasn't it? He would prove he didn't need *them* or *anyone*. And yet painful voices whirled, building a dichotomous storm. Between netting a game-winning shot to crippling losses, Peter succumbed to a tradition of sipping red street wine to celebrate or drown out the sorrows.

There were supposed to be many possibilities for him, but were there? Or would he end up like his father? Was he destined to become something he despised?

Peter knew he was woven into his performance. He couldn't free himself. Performing well warmed him with confident bravado, while underperforming shackled him to self-focused apathy. "Self-sabotage" were the words that came to his mind. No matter how fast he drove, he found himself with toxic mindsets caught up. He also tried to find stability on those roads, namely with his ex-girlfriend, who had grown exhausted by his self-deprecating attitude. She, too, was gone. If he were looking back on his life, she wasn't even on the horizon of his rearview mirror.

So consumed by his thoughts, Peter was surprised to feel the crimson glare of sunset. He realized how exhausted he was. With no conclusions to his worries, he sought distraction in music and driving his beloved car – at least the mirage of going somewhere new felt good.

Peter's Camaro was his prized possession. Its exterior glistened, polished, and preened. His obsessive approach kept the car safe from unconscientious drivers who parked too close. A bucket of polishers, snow foam ceramic coating, and clay bars sat waiting in his trunk. The engine purred like a kitten but was as fierce as a lion.

Peter loved to roar past the slow souls in the right lane.

The interior was a beautiful contradiction. The seats were torn, dashboard cracked, and the windows fogged often. Usually, the electrical system would flash warnings, but he ignored them. Peter's energy was focused on what others saw externally: his appearance, posture, and stature. No one ever saw the internal truth, the inner turmoil.

Gassing the 1044-mile journey in one day proved easy with radio blaring. It threw him off when his GPS's *Bing!* rang, "You have arrived at your destination."

Pretty impressive, Peter mused.

The Bluffs was a small, odd town on the outskirts of nowhere. It had old buildings, lonely streets, and greyscale décor – far from bright town lights. Anxiously grabbing the gear shift as he pulled downtown, Peter fired up a thin veil of self-mantra: "This is just a stop, not my destination."

Maybe, just maybe, there was a path to the League in this dank town. His first stop was the Speedsters team center. He got the keys to his one-bedroom 500sf apartment next to Cold Springs Liquor & Convenience, which he passed on the way to the grocery store. After unloading the groceries in his new pre-furnished pad, which made a local motel look 5-star extravagant, he crashed in uneasy anticipation of tomorrow's first practice.

The pace would be intense: two grueling daily practices for ten days straight, all in prep for the new season. It was a test of mental fortitude and resolve. Peter strung together a few impressive sessions that flashed his potential but followed them with hall-of-fame duds.

Plagued by his inconsistencies, training camp crowned Peter as a cheerleader at the end of a crowded bench. He practiced for three hours and recovered in his furnished prison cell. Road trips included games, hotels, sleeping, flying, and travel. No fanfare, lights, or glory. It was just a daily grind – day after day after day.

On top of the lonely grind, the professional world was cold, and no antifreeze was available. His close-knit team experiences at college were nonexistent, and the brotherhood he craved didn't exist. Everyone was focused on their own best interests. Conflicts and strife being the daily bread.

Isolated.

Disconnected.

Alone.

Peter longed for something firm to grasp onto.

Three months into the forgettable season, nothing changed except the worn-down padding of his bench seat. Unable to find relief in his love of playing, the nightlife's voice came calling. If it wasn't the nightlife, it was the liquor store.

Peter knew *life* was overtaking him. He thought no one noticed, but surely no one really cared either. It was as if he were on a battlefield, alone, surrounded by enemies.

The goal, his dream, the glory... and the very scope of his identity seemed blurred through his foggy windshield. The empty nights spent scrolling his phone and staring at the ceiling were filled with unanswerable questions: *Is this worth it? What is life truly about? Who am I really?*

On a fast track to nowhere, Peter left his apartment one frigid winter night, trying to silence the voices again. With all gas and no brakes, he floored it out of the Bluffs, unsure if he would ever return. Something was missing.

The vortex deepened as the night gave way to the crack of dawn.

Peter drove on until the first glimmer of light radiated like a halo on the sign ahead:

WELCOME TO UVILLE

Where *U Are Found*

Welcome to Uville

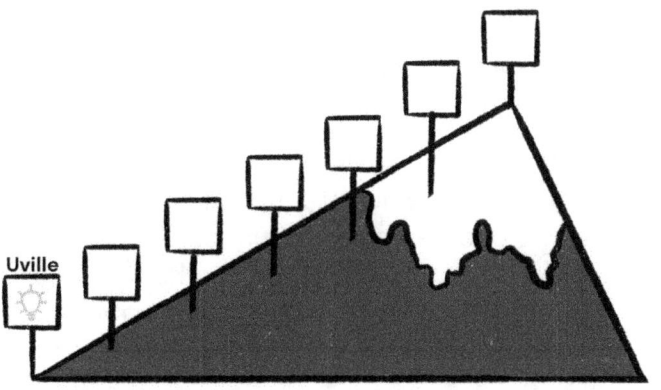

The engine gasped on fumes as Peter fixed his gaze on the slogan:

Where U are Found

Perhaps this was a sign, though he didn't believe in that sort of thing. But desperation had him longing for one. He coasted to the nearest gas station just as his beloved Camaro juddered to a stop.

Peter filled her up, wiped away the grime plastered to his windshield, and checked the cans of antifreeze. Nearly empty. He cranked up his beloved and slid into a side street parking spot. Shoved his hands into his pockets and walked until he came upon a bustling plaza downtown. There, he grabbed a double espresso and set out to explore the sights and sounds of Uville.

Perhaps, to find himself... he had to be lost.

The patrons at the local coffee shop were engrossed in their laptops, only pausing to down their mochas. The suits strutted through the open plaza with phones clamped to their ears as they fought against the chilly swirling winds. Never stopping. Just weaving through human traffic. There were kids at the bus stop, wrapped in scarves, staring at their screens.

The men playing basketball at the park caught his attention. They darted up and down the court clothed in heavy sweatsuits. The game abruptly ended at a standstill as they cursed at each other over a silly foul. The brief quiet gave rise to morning hustlers jamming their horns as they fought for prime parking spaces.

And yet the lasting image that throttled Peter was a middle-aged man brandishing his fist at a woman who'd taken his parking spot.

The angry man's face disgruntled Peter. As he watched him storm away, he turned his attention to the faces of other Uvillians watching. The people were disconnected, stoic, pensive, and void of joy. The burden on their faces, something he was all too familiar with, frightened him. So, he shoved his empty espresso cup into the bin and wandered for some time into the town.

As the sky deepened and Peter went on through the streets, he heard a young girl's sharp cry for her mom. He watched her stamping her foot, mittens shaking at her sides. Many ignored her, and others seemed annoyed she was causing a scene. Clearly they saw her as nothing more than an inconvenience to their self-obsessed misery.

Uville didn't seem any dissimilar from the rest of his world. It was another town where nothing significant existed.

He had seen enough. It was time to go. But where? The obvious choice was to quench his internal thirst with his favorite Southern Comfort and Coke before heading to nowhere. Peter found a bar, ducked inside, and found a cozy corner beside the heater.

With ice clinking his glass, he looked up at the television hanging above the bar. A headline flashed, "UVILLE MAYOR UNDER INDICTMENT!" And then a news reporter sat at her desk, proclaiming, "Up next, the town's mental health is in decline, and smash-and-grab crimes are on the rise. We will be right back with the full stories after the break."

After knocking back his drink, Peter skipped dinner and stumbled into the dank, misty night. He wandered north, bypassing a gloomy plaza. It was empty. Quiet. Yet Peter's mind whirled. Perhaps it was time to let basketball go. And do what? What else made him feel so good? The highs were exhilarating, and the lows were... low.

Peter wandered through the somber darkness, the ends of his toes numb from the biting cold. He'd transitioned from idea to idea, reflecting on mistakes that always seemed to work out. And yet... it wasn't enough. Surely, everything would work out if he stuck with what he knew. Right?

He staggered deep into the frosty dusk, clouded, confused, and with a heavy heart. The sky grew overcast until the shadows had no end or beginning. He was derailing and fast... and the cold was freezing him stiff.

As he drifted through the streets of Uville, Peter lifted his head and noticed he was standing at a unique crossroads. He was standing at the intersection of *Nowhere Street* and *Someday Avenue*. The oddity spoke as he turned to peek down *Someday Avenue*. A flickering light was several hundred yards down the lit path, glimmering enough to pierce through the cold haze.

What was that light in the darkness? Was it a sign? His heart thudded. The mere thought of crossing that precipice stifled him. Perhaps *Someday Avenue* would offer answers or new possibilities, but was he willing to take the first step?

After a long pause, Peter overcame his inertia and made his move. He stumbled down *Someday Avenue*. What came into focus was a sign reading:

MPA

Room Available

Perplexed, yet sparked by curiosity, he crept toward the entrance. Trembles ran up his arms as he dared hope that the next door may be the one... the one he had been looking for his entire life.

As he cracked it open, he was engulfed by the light radiating through the atrium. Warmth filled the lobby. He paused with a deep sigh and scanned the room. The walls showcased signed portraits and photographs of previous guests. Each picture showed the same strong-jawed, soft-eyed man standing beside them, illuminated by divine light.

Peter glanced at a couple laughing as they sat on a couch against the far wall. He wondered why they were so happy. His shoulders started to lift as he made his way to the opening desk. He became aware of an uncomfortable, uncommon feeling of openness. It was foreign, yet it felt good.

The attendant smiled. "Thanks for coming in tonight. It's pretty cold out there. Did you find our place, ok?"

Peter shrugged, "I found you by accident. I was about to high-tail it out of here."

"Sounds like your time didn't go as planned," he said. "Can I get you something to drink?"

"Sure, that would be great. Just nothing spicy."

The attendant went around the corner before reappearing with a steaming, round cup of hot chocolate. Thick, white cream swirled a peak, sprinkled with chocolate shavings and brown sugar syrup. Peter took a gulp and laughed at the warm sweetness. "Oh, my favorite," he said. "That was amazing and much appreciated." He put the cup down and used the same hand to greet the attendant. "I am Peter."

"Jhonny," the stranger replied. "I help run this place." He cast a sweeping glance around the room and when the couple noticed, they waved at him brightly. Jhonny returned his gaze to Peter. "What are you doing here?"

Peter took another sip. "Where should I begin?"

"When did your journey?"

"Well..."

Peter divulged his journey to Uville. Minutes slipped into an hour. Peter had no plans to stay in Uville, but the longer he spoke, the more Jhonny was drawn in. It was as if Peter truly mattered, and he felt like he did for the first time in a long while.

But it was getting late, and they were strangers. Why was this guy so interested in him? Jhonny exhumed fascination. He had true sincerity and yet supernal confidence that was undeniable. As if sensing Peter's uncertainty, Jhonny clapped his hands together. "Well," he said. "The night is getting long. Would you like to stay and rest up?"

"Here?" Peter blinked.

"Yes, the MPA. There is room."

Peter hesitated. He should have been exhausted, ready to pass out, but Jhonny energized him. "What does MPA stand for anyway?"

"Everyone gets around to that question," Jhonny said. "It stands for Max-Potential Academy."

Raising a brow, Peter asked, "Academy? Isn't this a Bed & Breakfast?"

"Technically, we are both. We keep an open door for people like you seeking respite," Jhonny said. "We are also an open door for those seeking opportunity."

"What type of opportunity are we talking about? Is this some weird cover-up scam?"

Jhonny replied, "I assure you we are 100% legit. You see, we serve a great organization motivated to change the world we influence. This is just one branch of our team."

Peter looked around the lobby and saw the couple sharing something funny on their phone.

Behind him Jhonny said, "We are experts in helping people grow strong in life and leadership to fulfil their maximum potential purpose."

"And you think I have that potential?" Peter turned to him once more, remembering the unworthiness he felt driving away from his childhood home. "Me?"

"We have a great track record of success, which I can attest to, having been through the program myself. We take pride in getting remarkable results."

"But I'm nobody... I just sit on the bench."

Jhonny raised a brow. "You matter as much as anyone else. Don't believe me? I hope you had a chance to look at the testimonies on the wall."

Peter scratched his head as he flickered to look at the photographs surrounding him. "So, what does this academy do?"

"Well, we help people get what they want. We help clarify your purpose and develop strong, anchored convictions that will support your mission. We help you find you so you can change the world you influence."

"That's cool," said Peter with wide eyes. "I had no idea a place or academy like this existed." MPA was sounding like music to his desperate ears. He knew he wasn't clear on his mission or purpose – or what *someday* could look like for his life. Life had to be more than work, playing basketball, and seeking pleasure. Perhaps MPA held the answers that could scratch his internal restless itch. Jhonny's hook was reeling him in.

"So, what makes you different?" Peter asked.

"Let's start at the beginning – with you. We provide coaching, training, and education on the fundamentals needed to ensure you can navigate your mission and be a great 21st-century leader. The fundamentals make all things possible and allow the best version of you to come forth," Jhonny declared.

"I have spent too much time trying to figure me out," Peter mused.

Jhonny laughed. "Well, Uville is a purgatory of sorts. It is where self-focused suffering exists as restless souls seek to find their way to their higher level or calling. The truth is that you can elevate yourself out of the matrix by gaining clarity."

Peter sat in the revelation and absorbed the wisdom.

"Now, the first growth step in MPA is gaining clarity and convictions on you. We believe greatness starts with U! You are uniquely created, wonderfully made, and distinct from anyone else. Your life is significant, and your talents matter. A beautiful combination of potential humanity and divinity merged into one. All the Power for You to succeed starts within, ready to be unlocked."

Peter leaned into every word as he spoke. Each word elevated the growing hope within. He had wondered if the front door would be the one to lead him on the right path. It seemed it was. And it was more than that. Humanity and divinity? The thought never crossed his mind, but he was fully aware that he lacked awareness on what that meant.

Jhonny continued, "The team here at MPA just believes Uville is a microcosm of the world. When everything is self-focused, selfishness and self-serving dominate your mindset... and darkness overcomes."

"The message becomes confusing for me. So how does MPA solve that problem?"

Jhonny clasped his hands. "The truth we teach in the Academy is self-focus chokes out your growth potential. Its cancerous growth leaves you disillusioned, disconnected and derailed in life. You start by clarifying who you are and developing an anchored identity. The focus then shifts to understanding your mission's impact on the world you influence. Then, going out to do it."

"That clarity sounds like water on a distant shore. I often feel like I am drowning. And when I swim, I am not confident in which direction I should be headed," Peter murmured, surprised by his transparency.

A long pause ensued as Peter reflected on his journey. Deep within, he felt an uncomfortable yet pleasant stirring that moved him toward Jhonny's message. Suddenly, his pupils enlarged, and his eyebrows raised. Discomfort revealed, and a realization came forth. He was engulfed in his own burning fire, trapped in his own Uville matrix. His goals, dreams, and relationships were centered on his desires and rewards.

At that moment, his internal self-convicting autopilot voice blared his familiar download: It's your shot, your chance to shine, your glory. Prove everyone wrong.

His shoulders slumped as he pressed his hands to his eyes. Regret ravished his mind. All of time stood still.

Jhonny seemed attuned to Peter's shift in countenance. He said, "What is coming to your mind about MPA?"

"Well, it's not so much MPA, but my coach used to call it the 'Me-Disease.'" His voice was hoarse with memory. "A disease possessed by self-interest and self-preservation... ruining the team. I can hear this voice inside me, sabotaging me."

Peter's hands found the strength to wipe his tears. Such remorse... the family, friends, and teammates he had hurt, alienated, and disappointed. Coming to terms with the deep-rooted impact of his self-focus proved a heavy cross to carry.

The slivers of the *Me-Disease* burned in the pits of his fire.

Peter Meets Coach G

Jhonny stepped toward Peter, wrapping an arm around him. Although it should have been awkward, Jhonny's presence soothed him.

Peter lifted his head, "I didn't see that coming," he confessed. "The last time I recall crying was when my brother gut-punched me. I guess I forgot how to – even how to feel."

Jhonny's eyes glistened, "Sounds like you've had it pretty difficult."

With a shrug, Peter didn't want to dwell on admitting anything yet. No one had listened before and it was strange to relax or believe Jhonny. "Tell me then," Peter pressed, "about MPA. I want the support if there is a clear path to help me live and reach my potential."

Jhonny said, "The first step is to connect you with Coach G, our leader and founder."

"Why do you call him Coach G?"

"Over time, the team would joke how 'good' he was at coaching. They started calling him Coach G, and it stuck."

"When can I meet him?"

Jhonny grinned. "Pull out your phone, and I will text you a link so you can hear his introduction to Max-Potential Academy. Grab a seat and watch. The video is part of the introductory online course in the Academy. It is called *The Power of U!*. It will give you a feel for his coaching style. Listen, and let me know if Max-Potential Academy is really for you."

"Sounds good." Peter sank into the couch, catching the couple's eye once more. They smiled, but Peter wasn't quite ready to feel settled there yet. He wondered if the couple were part of MPA. What had the program done for them? He managed a contrived head nod. Perhaps MPA and Coach G could help him find himself, gain a fresh start, or even get his professional goals back on track to the League. A spark was catching inside. He looked down from the couple, feeling the possibilities of a new *someday* were warming his frosted self-limiting beliefs.

When Peter clicked the link and heard Coach G's voice, he knew it was something special. Coach G spoke with transcendent strength and majesty:

"Hey, I am Coach G, and it's *GrowthTime!* I am the coach leader of Max-Potential Academy. If you are listening to this, you have met one of my representatives in the field. You are someone who longs for more in... and out of your life. The good news is that MPA is committed to your personal growth and development. It is the reason why we exist.

"To put you at ease, this isn't a get-rich or get-fixed-up quick internet scam. Personal growth isn't easy, but it is the pathway to fulfillment and results. There will be sacrifices and difficult changes you will need to make to reach your potential. Be confident we offer a safe, non-judgmental place to gain the clarity and convictions that will anchor your journey... allowing your confidence to soar and you to overcome this world."

"Now, part of this introduction to MPA offers real-world coaching, a little flavor to jumpstart your journey. Just press pause and reflect on what you learned in Uville and where you need growth."

Peter hit "pause." Lost in the U of Uville, he needed clarity.

So, he pressed "play" again.

Coach G's emphatic voice emerged, "The place of power I would like to share is a coaching tool that will begin the process of gaining clarity on the *Power of U!* Your unique *Purpose Plan*. What you do, how you do it, and why you do it sets you apart from the crowd of life. It helps define your humanity. Here is a simple visual representation for you."

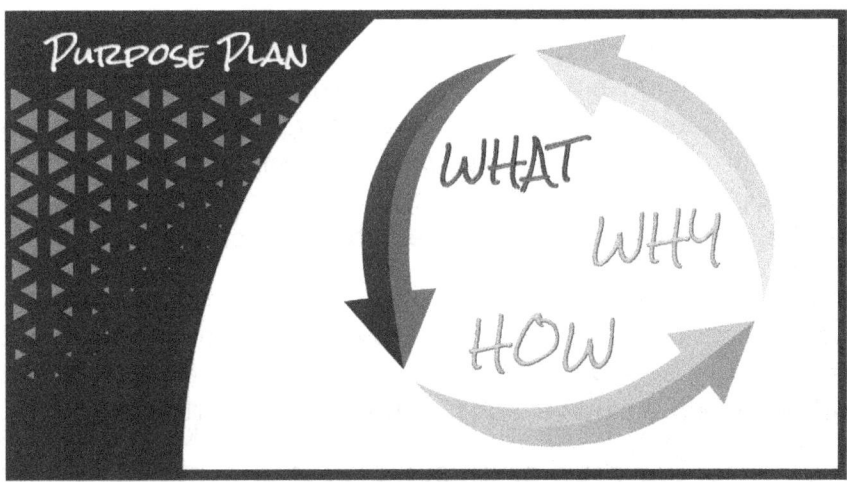

Coach G continued, "Once you embrace truth, there is a purpose and a plan for your life; the next step is to unlock your *Purpose Plan*. We at team MPA are here to help you define your WHAT as your mission. Your HOW as your highest values. Your WHY as your specific unique motivation. You probably already have some ideas, but clarity is king. Realizing your purpose plan is like building a wheel: each component slots together, the wheel runs smooth, turning over, and over, gaining momentum. It runs fast. You move faster. You travel further."

Coach G's message was soul food. Perhaps that was the value of MPA... to help guide him through the vast uncharted space of himself.

"But let's go deeper," Coach G continued. "Let me plant an uncomfortable seed that has never had a chance to bloom. Being 'created' means you originated from a Divine higher power and were made in the likeness and image of that power. And that Divine relationship, and access to the Divine nature, needs to be clarified for you to allow the full 100% *Power of U!* to be manifested.

"Yes, I realize all the negative connotations, resistance and ugly history that will present itself, but gaining clarity on why you were created, how the Divine sees you, and what He expects are the spokes on the wheel of your *Divine Purpose Plan*."

Peter hit a stop. He possessed jaded views regarding religion and all the quirky spiritual people he knew. His philosophy was to go to church twice a year to appease his conscience in case there was a God or Divine higher power. Yeah, he would admit to throwing up a desperation prayer or two, but he was convinced they simply traveled through the outer realms.

It was difficult enough to figure life out without introducing a contentious idea. And yet Coach G's words echoed: "Growth isn't easy." Perhaps his *Divine Purpose Plan* was wrapped in real truth. Maybe it held the power and potential to elevate his confidence.

After all, if Peter could have figured it out by himself, then why hadn't he?

Coach G continued, "Be confident we will help you navigate that difficult yet empowering self-discovery road. Before we connect on how MPA works, let's coach one step further. A pitfall that needs to be exposed about U. Distortion comes when you become intoxicated with your individuality and shift the exclusive focus to your needs.

"The *Power of U!* is meant to be used to change the world you influence. I realize the conundrum, the existing oxymoron. It would be best to embrace your uniqueness, yet you cannot be the focus. Your gifts aren't meant to be idolized but given away."

Peter reflected on this. How many gifts had he received in this life? People. Personality. Health. Athletics. He had lathered in belongings and experiences, chosen his vanity over the needs of others. All along... he had been idolizing the wrong things.

Then Coach G posed, "Let's shift gears. The leading question to reflect on is what keeps people jailed in the purgatory of U?"

Peter eased back.

As if knowing the truth, Coach G said, "Yes, you probably have pinpointed the greatest barrier to your growth and development. It is the pathogen to a distorted U, the Pride-Ego! The simple version is pride says, 'I am right' and 'My way is right' even if I am wrong. The inflated ego elevates yourself above others and the mission. The Pride-Ego is the worst virus inherent to man."

The truth bomb exploded in Peter's heart. He knew. Coach G's words just brought to light – the resistance, the stubbornness, the fake "I-need-to-know-it-all" attitude he was clothed in. Coach G called out the virus, front and center. Yet, the virus was a contagion.

Peter paused, gazed high at the glowing colorful atrium, and held his chin up with the palm of his hand. He wondered how he could overcome it.

The
Decision

P eter enjoyed the uncomfortable stretch of being challenged. If anything, he had proved over the years he wouldn't back down. He pressed play to hear Coach G say, "The cure is death to self. Yes, a virus must die for life and vitality to come forth. Realize the Pride–Ego is never satisfied. It always hungers and longs for more to stay alive. More recognition, more judgment, more self-validation, more success. More. More. More. It *must* be put to death, through surrender and humility, for true growth and your highest potential."

Peter straightened. How often had he sought more? To satisfy the requirement of the Pride–Ego... *More* felt good at the moment but never left him good. The uncomfortable words "surrender" and "humility" echoed through the fog of his mind.

For the first time, he could see the work ahead. And it began in Uville.

Coach G returned to say, "The core of MPA is a coaching program designed to equip you with the life and leadership skills to be successful on your mission. There is a playbook, online courses, access to coaches, weekly motivation, online webinars, 'Ask the Coach' sessions, one-on-one coaching, and an online community of like-minded MPAs. All are put in place to provide the guidance, accountability and support you will need to succeed.

"Thank you for taking the time to learn about MPA, and hopefully, you found this time a valuable investment into your growth. Your representative will give more details and answer any questions about starting your growth journey. Remember, *U Matter* and people need you to live to your max–potential. Let's go change the world together," Coach G concluded as a bright light panned.

Peter exhaled as he sat forward in the chair. It was a surreal, transcendent promise. Coach G was helping him find himself in the hope of a reimagined future.

As he rested his elbows on his knees, dreams floated in. Images of his family, friends, teammates, and even the people of the world flashed through his cerebral cortex. His emotions started to bubble. Maybe, just maybe, he could change the world. Maybe he was created to use his gifts to influence others.

But...

He could still feel the burn marks on his back. Was this just another flawed, failed leader in his path? A villain? Or was he willing to trust Coach G and team MPA? Did they present a clear path toward unlocking his potential? Was he willing to embrace the growth journey out of his forsaken, distorted Uville?

Pushing his hand into his hair, he stared at his Nike trainers. Suddenly, he heard a sound... music. The song that sparked his engine on many cold nights: *"You only get one shot. Opportunities come once in a lifetime..."* The melody echoed from the desk.

Peter rose and strode with heroic intentionality across the room. There was Jhonny, who stood waiting. Peter looked at him and asked, "How do I sign up for this academy? How much does it cost?"

Beaming, Jhonny exclaimed, "Well, that is awesome to hear! I will share that MPA is an exclusive program, so it does come with an investment. The membership commitment is $10,000. The investment includes access to the online course, MPA coaching sessions, webinars, tools, and resources. It also allows lifetime access to the community and Coach G's training. Does that work for you?"

Peter flinched. His eyes bulged in discouragement as he began to rub his forehead, searching for a response. All the initial courage eviscerated. He knew he didn't have the resources to join this team. He played in the Bluffs, where minor league money was living check-to-check.

"Jhonny..." he hummed, "that investment is significantly beyond my means. I am afraid I will have to pass."

When he lifted his gaze, Jhonny's possessed eyes of holy fire locked onto his, and with a voice of passion spoke into the dark, "Peter, I realize the investment is high. I will follow my intuition that there is something special about you."

"Me?"

"Yes, you. We will offer you a sponsorship for the MPA team. Consider it a scholarship."

"That's incredible," he breathed.

"I have an unction. You are going to do something amazing."

"I will." Peter nodded. "I will do something amazing."

Jhonny inclined his head. "You are accepted onto team MPA."

An odd cocktail of elation and resistance swallowed Peter. He reasoned that this must be his first test. Humbly accept or hold onto his Pride-Ego, taking nothing from no one? He was overwhelmed and touched that someone *believed* in him. Gathering his emotions and tilting his squared jaw, he knew the curse of his Pride-Ego would take an overdue break today.

Jhonny came from behind the desk with his arms wide. And Peter went straight into them.

"Jhonny," Peter said. "I don't know what to say. Thank you. Thank you. I will give you my best and attack this academy with all my heart."

Jhonny pulled back, hands on Peter's shoulders. "I am counting on it," he said. "Now, get some rest tonight. There is added growth work to finish course: *#1. The Power of U!* Here is an access code to start your online account and download the app. You will be able to review the Team MPA handbook. It will be your study guide. Inside the app, you must activate notifications and calendars to access the online webinars, 'Ask the Coach' sessions, one-on-one coaching sessions, and connect with the online community of like-minded MPAs.

"Even better, we recently launched Rubystar, Coach G's virtual assistant. It can be accessed 24/7 via phone, text, or the Internet. It links right into your car navigation system or within the app. Rubystar has a straight line of communication with Coach. Best part? Coach G will be watching over your entire growth journey."

Peter nodded, patting the phone in his pocket. "Will do, Jhonny." As he turned and headed for the door toward the stairwell, he turned and asked, "Hey, you are an amazing representative for MPA. How come you care so much and know so much about Coach G?"

Jhonny smiled. "Oh, I am the Coach's son – a player and a coach."

Peter grinned from ear to ear. He could see the resemblance in their smiles. What were the chances, the impossible odds, of him meeting this Coach G and his son in the dark of Uville?

He saw the sign. It came into full view as he settled into the first restorative sleep he could recall.

The sun shone brightly the next day, and life felt wholesome. Peter crossed *Nowhere Street*. Under the dazzling sunlight, the winter air seemed warmer, and he adjusted his sunglasses with a playful smirk. Even Uville seemed brighter... cleaner.

Peter noticed a man in a suit stopping to change an elderly woman's tire, a woman smiling at the bus stop to those who were disgruntled, and two kids stopping their phone-scrolling long enough to notice a pregnant woman needing help loading her groceries.

As Peter stood in the café, the barista who'd brewed his espresso last night spotted him immediately. "Peter, right?" she sprigged. "Double-shot on me!"

Afterwards, he listened to the urge to stop and encourage a young boy practicing hoops on the courts before heading out. Uville felt newfangled, filled with possibilities and opportunities. He was lighter, his lenses cleaner, and a renewed hope warmed him more than the noonday sun.

As he climbed into his Camaro, he noticed the inside had shifted. The rips were thinner, the dashboard shinier, and the foggy window was beginning to clear up.

MY GROWTHTIME!

COACH Q

It is time to take a pit stop on the road. This section invites you to join the growth journey. Meaningful growth begins when you ask the right, powerful questions. Powerful questions send us to the unknown, where we search for answers. The unknown can be uncomfortable and terrifying, but we gain clarity by exploring ourselves and digging deep.

True growth starts with self-awareness. Through seeking clarity, you unlock yourself and allow new possible truths to come forth. Embracing new truths serve your best life, moving you towards developing strong convictions. These convictions propel you into life-changing actions elevating your confidence.

The upside is that you will reduce stress, anxiety, and the darkness that comes with being unclear on your *Purpose Plan*. A fresh love for you and others will emerge.

Fulfillment, purpose, and passion – your best life starts with this first growth zone, the ***Power of U!***

This is the simple formula:

Clarity → Convictions

Convictions → Confidence

Clarity + Convictions + Confidence = Unlimited potential

SELF-ASSESSMENT

This is a short clarity assessment for you to begin to unlock the *Power of U!* The scale is 1 – 10 (10 being crystal clear and 1 being clear as mud).

1. *How clear are you on WHAT your mission in life is?* [   ]

2. *How clear are you on your WHY? (a clear vision/ motivational statement)* [   ]

3. *How clear are you on HOW your top three core values operate?* [   ]

4. *How clear are you on the Divine Purpose plan for your life?* [   ]

5. *How clear are you on WHY God created you?* [   ]

6. *How clear are you on WHAT the Divine expects of you?* [   ]

7. *How clear are you on HOW the Creator sees you?* [   ]

If the answers are cloudy (less than 8), then that is where the growth work needs to occur. If it takes you a long time to articulate your thoughts, you find yourself searching, grasping, or formulating the answers as you go... you are cloudy. This is ok. That is why you are reading this!

GROWTHTIME

Let's begin the journey to unlock your *Purpose Plan:*

Courage to confront the Pride-Ego Virus:

1. What areas of your Life and Leadership have been affected by your Pride-Ego?

    (List specific examples that have hindered your growth in relationships, leadership and with the Divine)

2. What steps of humility will you take to make things right?

What is your WHAT mission?

Grab your *My GrowthTime! journal* – a notebook specifically marked for your personal growth. Schedule an hour block of undistracted time to reflect on the following questions. Write out anything and everything that comes to mind. Don't prequalify your thoughts or hopes—get them all out. Dream big.

- What is your Big WHAT – your mission?
- What do you hope will happen Someday in your life?
- If money were not a limiting concept, what risk would you take?
- What impact do you hope your business will make Someday?
- What impact will your Someday have on others' lives?
- What would be the best part of Someday coming to fruition? (How would you feel?)

Next step... marinate in your answers for 7 days. Then repeat the exercise above – this allows for increased vision and insight.

Clarity on your *Divine Purpose Plan*:

Take the bold step to gain clarity on one of the *Divine Purpose Plan* questions asked above in the assessment. Reflect, seek, read, Google, ask friends, and pray with an open mind and willing heart over the next seven days – intentionally set aside a minimum of 20 minutes each day. Write out all your thoughts. After 7 days, take note of 3 convictions that came to clarity.

Example: How does the Divine see me?

1.

2.

3.

ENCOURAGEMENT

Writing and journaling are powerful tools for removing mind clutter, gaining clarity, and allowing possibilities to be birthed into the tangible realm. The actions above are a starting point! Realize more growth work will be needed to unlock the *Power of U!* Don't take the shortcut; growth isn't easy. Put in the work!

Additional resources are available at mygrowthtime.com

THE POWER OF BELIEFS

The Road to the League

P eter knew he had unfinished business in the Bluffs. No longer driving like a bat out of hell, he played a shuffle of soft classic rock and allowed his hopes to wander. What could Someday look like? What else was possible? He could use basketball as a platform to serve others. He could start a mentorship program or run clinics and camps to help youngsters. He could start a non-profit for disenfranchised youth like himself. Or what if he created a website with resources to help kids from troubled families?

His story could serve as an inspiration to motivate others to reach their potential. Each idea brought life. Each thought slowly suffocated the desire to be so self-focused.

The next day, Peter crushed practice. He shot lights-out, played outstanding defense, and rallied his teammates past the grind. Perplexed by the resurgence, even his nemesis teammate joked about what special juice he had sipped on before practice.

And to everyone's surprise, he stayed hot, stringing together an intense week of practice.

The good news was that the Bluffs' head coach took notice and recognized him as "Player of the Week" despite him not playing one minute in the games. Peter's gait was transforming – a little extra humble strut.

After practice or on road trips, he dug into the *Power of U!* course outlined. He identified a list of his highest values, as Coach G said, "Your HOW of the *Purpose Plan*." It was clever how Coach

G linked your top three values to being your North Star, guiding you in making daily decisions. The more choices Peter made aligning with his values, the more confident he felt.

It wasn't smooth sailing as his limitations and Pride-Ego were formidable opponents. At least the path to change was clearing up, as he often reflected. With new anchors to his identity coming into his being, he explored gaining awareness of the Divine. He leaned into Team MPA's online resource, "A Coach's Perspective on the *Divine Purpose Plan*." It proved highly uplifting and brought new truths into his light. He scribed the first convictions that had begun to crystalize:

- ✓ He was created for relationship and purpose
- ✓ He was loved as a son of the Divine
- ✓ He was expected to learn and follow the Divine's ways

Infatuation seeped into Peter. The simple, transitional impact of being intentional with his personal growth only further distanced himself from his old ways. His self-focused attitude slumped in the backseat. Mistakes and failures slid off his shoulders. The choice to kick the bottle became easier.

He fell in love with a profound proverb in the Bible-thick manuscript called the MPA playbook:

He who refreshes others will himself be refreshed.

The truism moved his mindset to great gain. First, he befriended any grocery store clerk, then showed kindness to the team bus driver, and followed that up injecting laughter into a frazzled airline attendant.

The proverb's wisdom didn't stop there. Rather than use his quick wit to make teammates or friends the butt of jokes, Peter used his gift to encourage them. Now, going the extra mile with the knuckleheads on the Speedsters he despised... that was a tall task. Yet, stepping into their world broke down barriers and opened the space to uplift them.

The proverb proved true. The more he gave, the better he felt. The more he refreshed others, the more revitalized he became. Peter could taste the difference. His response to conflict improved, relationships smoothed, and his self-awareness grew. The *Me-Disease* was losing its power.

Peter even crossed a once unthinkable broken bridge: his relationship with his father. The rightful rage was laid to rest upon Peter's self-awareness that he, too, had failed as a son. He hadn't been perfect, and yet, why was he holding his father to an inflated standard? The lessons of MPA helped him see that behind the veil of alcohol was the Pride-Ego virus. That was the pathogen shredding his childhood.

Through a stomach-nauseating call home, Peter took that courageous step. With his voice quivering and heart pounding, he confronted the pain of the past and sought a new beginning. Silence and sobs filled the call. Peter heard his dad cry for the first time.

It was a whirlwind blizzard paradox. In the cold of winter, Peter was blooming. No longer a disgruntled partner on the bench, he was the motivator. He sought consistent feedback, updated his nutrition program and rest routines, tweaked his shooting form, and invested time into studying scouting reports. With extra reps and double days in the weight room, Peter was on a revived mission to reach his potential.

Payday finally came. The coach started to give him minutes.

Now, the Speedsters were mired in a mid-season slump and in jeopardy of missing the playoffs for the first time in nine years. Even still, it was a complete surprise that early spring day, seven months into the season, when the Speedster's coach called him into his office. It was time for a shakeup. Peter would be starting the next game.

"You only get one shot to blow; this opportunity comes once in a lifetime."

To everyone's delight, Peter was the spark the Speedsters craved. It was an epic rally; they won eight of their last ten games to make the playoffs.

Peter's car accelerated through the turns. The standard v-6 Camaro engine was supercharged to the Z-28. He was playing lights-out as the playoffs approached; an unexpected coming-out party. He played his heart out, pressing the team to the conference finals before losing a nail-biter seven-game series to the eventual champion Skyforce.

The after-season party didn't stop. Peter was named one of 20 "Up and Coming Talents" in the Midwest Farm League and invited to a three-day elite showcase. All League scouts would be in attendance.

Peter vowed not to airball.

He put in extra reps and drilling sessions the month leading up to the showcase. The work paid off. His north star lit up the sky. His reward was a personal invite by the Wisconsin Antlers of the League. Now, it wasn't a coveted contract but an opportunity to travel with the Antlers' summer developmental team for a circuit of games. One step closer. Another shot to prove his value.

Each step was infused with confidence and power. Any feelings of being overwhelmed and outmatched were kicked to the curb. Peter brimmed with conviction... he belonged at the next level.

Then... *it* happened.

As the League season was about to begin and the offers were sent out, Peter got the call... one he had hoped for all his life. The call sent chills through his soul.

Peter signed a contract with the LA Shippers of the League. They had tracked his summer progress and swooped in on the Antlers, signing him to a one-year conditional contract.

Peter's joy was as deep as the ocean. His shout cracked the paint on his bedroom walls.

The song blared as he danced, *"You only get one shot to blow; this opportunity comes once in a lifetime."*

Only this time, the melody had a harmonious tone... and the contentious edge dissipated. Now, the celebration party didn't last very long as the season tipped off in six weeks. Peter pressed the pedal to the metal to transition to the West Coast. He was going to "La La Land," as he liked to call it — the town of glitz, glamor, and glory — a place that would challenge his mindset and heart's intent.

Peter was ready for it. He knew his identity was anchored in something far greater than himself. With Coach G's steady support and the MPA playbook in tow, a powerful compilation of truths and life experiences from past MPAs, he knew he was part of a championship team. The book was filled with wisdom and values so Peter concentrated on carrying them forward.

The Rubystar app was also a gem. With a unique, calming voice, she was quick to respond to any search request for tools or resources. She was a living podcast available on-demand. Through her, Jhonny dropped affirmations and wisdom, and the online community proved a powerful source of connection to like-minded individuals. There was also a growing network of local MPA gatherings to spur one another on — even in La La Land.

Goodness was bubbling forth... and Peter cherished soaking in its bath.

The Wheels of Change

The sky was crisp and clear on Peter's trip to La La Land. No burn marks or rubber were left behind; the sun radiated on the path ahead. He cranked the music of praise, a new song vibrating through the base, and set his cruise control on the open road.

The posh pad was quite the upgrade from the Bluffs, almost double in size. It was 20 minutes from the white sandy beaches, palm trees and ocean breeze.

Despite living in such a paradise, Peter was laser-focused on preseason training. The season was one month away, and he was brimming with anticipation to play for the Shippers. Riding high on the crests of life with the crisp, salty air, and caw of seagulls, he thought life couldn't be better until... his first MPA gathering at the local Tex-Mex restaurant. Luck? Divine coincidence? There he met Shannell.

Magic in a bottle.

She was unique and unlike any other woman he had ever met or laid his eyes upon. Her strong disposition meshed with an open, soft heart. Charismatic, funny, and driven, their worlds collided with fierce force. On the first day, their hands touched, a fiery energy manifested, igniting their unity. From that day on, if Peter wasn't training, he was with Shannell. Countless hours past the midnight strike, they laughed, shared their past pains, and dreamed of changing the world together. Endlessly squeezing every ounce of time together, it was a blink before they held each other's hearts in their hands.

It was a gift the Divine had granted, and it was unfathomable to foreshadow that Peter would be on one knee on those sandy beaches in just a few short months. It was an unfolding envisioned life together.

As the season began, Peter leveled up with the competition. Hustling, and doing the dirty work were his calling cards, along with a sweet jump shot. His voice hyped the veteran players as the team pressed through the mental grind of preseason two-a-days. Until...

Peter's ankle snapped.

It was an unapologetic, apocalyptic pop echoing through the gym. The players stopped and cringed. The feisty, competitive air was suctioned from the building. The General Manager dropped his phone.

Peter fell, grimacing as a shudder rippled through the crowd. All the players screeched to a halt. Pain. White-hot pain laced up Peter's leg. He fell, blurred by agony as the team gathered around him. There were hands on his shoulders and face. Someone was shouting. Soon, physicians sprinted to the basket, stabilizing the situation.

The afternoon was spent in the hospital running tests and X-rays. Cruel reality was made known. Peter was looking at six months of rehabilitation for a full recovery. His physical pain would subside in a few weeks, but Peter was choking on the emotional pill. He hadn't even made it past the preseason schedule.

The Shippers called him into the office the following week. A tough business decision had to be made to make room for able-bodied players. They were exercising the conditional part of his contract and releasing him from the team. The Shippers offered financial support, rehabilitation, and another opportunity to connect with the MFL... *if* he could endure the intense recovery ahead.

Peter's heart cracked. As an unproven player, he was expendable. His shoulders hung as he fought back tears. He thanked them, reached for his crutches, and limped down the long, dim hallway. Change opened another door.

The Max-Potential Academy community offered condolences and encouragement. Jhonny reached out. Coach G emailed a positive note on the power of perseverance. Peter felt the love from MPA and Shannell. Their support breathed wind into his sails.

Peter and Shannell's wedding was on the horizon, and her presence strengthened his resolve. He was determined to avoid retreating into his shell. Isolating wasn't an option; it was time to grow up. Besides, all the time to recover would give him and Shannell more time to build their story together.

Peter lived at the physical rehabilitation center. During the quiet hours, he flooded his mind with the Rubystar app's encouraging stories. His self-talk mantra rooted itself within... It was not the end but a bump on the road. Adversity struck all. It was how you responded that decided if you reached your potential.

Building mental muscle wasn't easy, but it was a far cry from going back to Uville. There was a greater purpose. He could find ways to make a positive impact. If he believed in MPA's mission to change the world he influenced, he couldn't quit.

No collapsing. No shooting an airball. His mission was on the line.

Peter beat all the odds. Four and a half months later, he was cleared to play basketball again. The good news was that the Shippers connected him with the Yacoma Royals in the MFL. After a quick tryout, he signed on to join the team mid-year.

Yacoma was another obscure town in the Pacific Northwest. Dank and dreary, the sky was at peace, clouding any sun rays. His new home was a dingy motel room just outside the town where they housed all the transit players. When he wasn't practicing, training, and traveling, Peter cuddled up reading and studying his playbook. He even burned through his data, Facetiming Shannell, who was staying in La La Land until things settled.

With just three months left in the season, Peter hoped to regain his form and secure another shot with the League. Week one: adapting. Week two: conditioning. Week three: playing rotation. By week five, Peter started to hobble. Both knees were inflicted with a dull, throbbing pain. He brushed it aside, ignoring the escalating symptoms in favor of doing what he loved. Just part of finding *my groove*, he reasoned. Athletes pushed through pain. The reasonable course of action was to manage the discomfort with ice and high dosages of Advil... and press on.

Yet, like a warped pair of car rotors, the screech and grind took their toll on his body. His play declined over the coming weeks. His warrior mentality crashed as the team doctor had a polarizing agenda. Unable to fully flex and straighten his knees just eight weeks back, Peter was overruled. Acute quad tendinitis with slight tears of the quad tendon in both knees was the official diagnosis. The prescription a four-month resting and recovery process.

It was a long-suffering summer offseason, physically and mentally. A harsh civil war divided his thoughts and drained his internal resources.

The voice of judgment, or the "Oppressor" as he liked to call it, always came to him. "You have failed," it said. "The league has passed you by. This isn't for you. Give up."

Another voice, the "General" he coined, would shoot back: "The Divine has a plan for you. Keep pressing forward, and don't look back. You are not a victim but a victor."

Blow for blow, the battle kept him on edge. Peter found awareness in moments of deep reflection. He sensed that his emotional range and motivation always followed the voices he heeded. Fear, disappointment, and anxiety always followed the Oppressor, who seemed hell-bent on warring against hope, positivity, and possibilities offered by the General.

It was an epic, bloody battle raging through many hot summer nights.

Further intensifying the battle was his financial drain, with money running scarce. Peter reflected on what life possibilities could look like without basketball. If he couldn't use basketball as a platform to change the world, then perhaps this was a sign to explore other options. Maybe it was time to hang up the sneakers. He had finished college, so perhaps he could pursue a new career.

Or stick it out one more time.

The new season would be there before he knew it. In a last–ditch effort, he staked his flag on the voice of hope strengthened by team MPA and Shannell. One last shot.

From the outside looking in, the League tarried for no one. Other prospects and new candy were always in their face. Out of sight, out of mind. Yet, he received a fortuitous bounce of the ball. One of his old assistants was now the coach of the Steers of Idaho in the MFL. He passed his physical and signed his contract.

It was a cloudy day as Peter and Shannell loaded up the car and made the 14-hour trek north to Potato Country. They had barely unpacked into their two-bedroom apartment and refilled the gas tank before the wheels of change ushered in insanity.

Upon his return to rigorous training, pain burned through in his lower back, setting fire down his lower left leg. The agony spiraled out of control over the coming weeks, often leaving him sprawled out on the carpet floor. No practice. No playing. Initially diagnosed as a minor strain with back spasms by the trainers, the doctor delivered a far more crippling. His back's neurological center was damaged and had succumbed to the pounding of the sport.

The MRI revealed his lower back vertebrae were in a bulging and degenerative state, the equivalent of a 70-year-old man. The heart knife prognosis was with six months of intense rehab; there was an optimistic chance he could walk and live pain-free with an outside chance to jog again.

It was those very words that cracked his skull. "Walk without pain! Is that how this ends?" Peter fired his disbelieving voice at the orthopedic specialist. His veins throbbed. The doctor had seen this before – the end of a dream.

As he fired out of the office into the open parking area, Peter looked high into the Heavens and shouted with clenched fists, "Is that what you have dealt me after all I have put towards my personal growth, our relationship, and this mission? How could you allow this to happen again? What the $%^&! is going on?"

He slammed the car door and sunk into the seat. Another blast of pain shot through his back. Anger and despair were a dangerous, glorious cocktail. He peeled rubber to nowhere, pounding the steering wheel and blowing up obscenities he had left behind. The internal rage blazed for hours... until he returned to his apartment. There, his head flopped into his chest, and his heart cried out to the Divine. *Does God really care?* He begged. *Why is this happening?*

The agonizing trek back home was stretched with unexpected curves, blurred lane lines, and potholes juddered along the way. Life was out of his control, and another pep talk on building character and perseverance in trials seemed like utter vomit.

Stuck in neutral?

No, his life was in reverse.

The following year was an utter survivalist's wilderness. Despite the optimistic efforts to follow the treatment plan, his condition regressed... His body was broken. His bank was broken. His future was broken.

Despite his best efforts to find the voice of growth, there were moments of regression. He took a passive approach to MPA, often disregarded Rubystar's notifications, and delayed responding to Coach G or Jhonny.

Where did the growth go? Why had it died?

Peter felt his convictions about MPA slipping. If Coach G desired to provide guidance and support, why was he so stuck? Maybe

MPA and this *Power of U!* weren't all they had promised. How could he change the world while nearly incapacitated? The thought even flashed into his mind: What if it was time to move on from team MPA?

Restless nights were worsened by an onslaught of woes: health, cash, life direction, and his relationship. Cracks formed between him and Shannell. Their once strong power of unity was breaking down.

Fear, failure, and self-doubt scratched him like thorns. He wondered if he would ever fulfill his potential and his ability to progress in Max-Potential Academy.

How would he even provide for a family? How could he overcome this suffering?

It was a battle of beliefs.

Crisis at Exitville

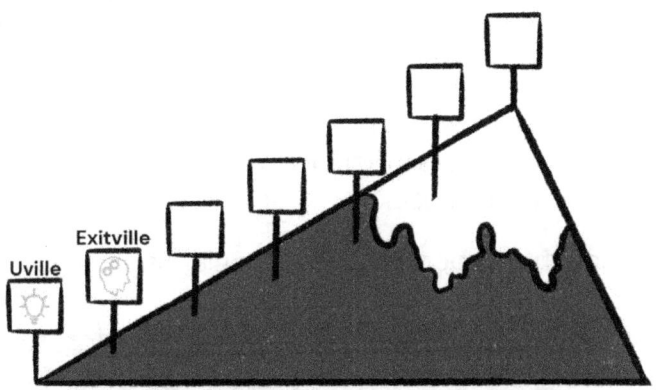

Peter's once-prized Camaro sputtered like an obsolete Plymouth station wagon. Beat up, gaskets blown, and chugging on fumes; he could barely slide into the car's seat. The daily trek to the physical therapist specialist proved futile, save the comfort that he was at least doing something.

The doctors had grown despondent as he fell into the minute percentage of individuals who didn't respond to treatment. How could he overcome these trials thrust upon him? What was his mission in this mess?

The wilderness grew, entangling, drawing him deep into a dark, feral quandary. Another day, another trek to the physical therapist office. Exiting Crown Valley Parkway, veering past the housing communities, a quick turn, and entering its parking lot. Every mind numbing trip down the road depleting his soul's energy.

On a breezy fall afternoon, Peter's normal route was oddly marked by a detour sign. With no construction ahead, he pinged on Rubystar.

Rubystar activated "Directions" with her silky voice, "Stay on course for the next 20 miles." Hesitant at the length of the detour, Peter asked Rubystar a second time, "Directions to the clinic."

Rubystar's response repeated, so he drove out through palm trees and communities that eventually gave way to the brushy tumbleweed blowing across this deserted path. As the road narrowed, cautionary cones and flashing lights lined the terrain.

With eyebrows furrowed and beads of sweat glistening, Peter decided Rubystar was misguided. Surely, he had missed something. It was time to turn back.

That thought evaporated when he glanced ahead:

Scratching his head, Peter had lost sense of his surroundings. He mused, *Who names a town "Exitville" anyway?*

A half-mile from Exitville, he slammed on the brakes as a band of tattered and torn warriors marched down the road in a defiant rage. Their rants grew louder as he approached the mass, "This sucks! We are not going to take it. No, we ain't going to take it. No more!"

The shouts reverberated through his windows as their furrowed, hardened faces never broke rhythm.

Peter swerved off-road through the brush to avoid confrontation before slamming the brakes to a halt. His car was left in a bowl of dust. Before it could settle, he was engulfed by a second, larger group that made the first group sound like a Sunday School choir. They chanted an angry song: "We are going back to Uville. Go back to Uville. We are going back to Uville."

Confused, Peter rolled down his window. But before any words came out, a man stuck his face before him, his breath nearly melting Peter's eyebrows. "Get out of here while you can!" he yelled. "It is insanity trying to pass through this town!"

Peter beamed the window up. The sound of bottles and rocks smashing against the road behind him escalated the tyranny.

With law and order gone, Peter peeled out, full gas, without understanding he was now on a direct course *into* Exitville. He coughed the dirt in his lungs and wondered how this place had turned into a war of the worlds.

Why was there an exodus? And what were these insurgents running from?

Curiosity and a slight fear of trying to reverse course kept Peter moving forward through the hysteria. Swerve. Veer left. Avoid debris. Moving slowly through the rubble as he arrived at the center of that demilitarized town. His eyes focused on two factions of people separated by industrial-roped lines. One group was irate and screaming obscenities at the other. Peter labeled this group the *"Haters"*. They seethed resentment and dripped anger through clenched teeth. Malcontents, their eyes sparkled with sadistic rejoicing, fascinated by their grumbling rhetoric.

The other group held their peace. Calmness was their mask as they talked to one another about what could be done. Peter called this group the *"Growers"*.

A voice appeared from the Haters. He declared, "We are never going to make it. This wilderness called Exitville is swallowing us up. We cannot overcome these barriers, detours, and obstacles." He brandished his fist. "This journey is filled with them. We have no resources, we are not strong enough to endure, and Coach's leadership has deserted us. This MPA is a lie!"

Another Hater screamed, "We are going to appoint a new leader. We need to rely on ourselves. This miserable road must end today. Let's pack up and join the wise ones headed back to Uville. Others feel free to stay in Exitville and make up your own rules. There is no getting through."

The Haters cheered with wild abandon. Some scurried off to join the exodus back to Uville. Others stood, mindset locked in, scouring for shelter to make sense of their hopeless madness.

The Growers pleaded with the Haters. They implored them to change their mindset and beliefs about this present adversity.

One voice from the Growers emerged, "We will not stop on our way to reach our potential. These obstacles, barriers and walls exist within us. They are our belief barriers. This present challenge reveals our beliefs about ourselves, our mission, and the leadership of our great organization, MPA. We choose to *grow* through this *adversity*. We need to *unify* with a singular mindset pushing forward."

Peter's heart thudded. The strength of the voice in crisis was gripping. He wanted to believe... but what was the voice of *growth* calling forth? And how could he choose between the separated battle ropes?

The Growers' voice sang, "This is our challenge to advance. We cannot embrace limiting beliefs about ourselves. Fear, self-doubt, and self-reliance are our enemies. These are the walls and obstacles restraining us."

The Haters paused as the dust settled before Peter's eyes.

"We will not be overtaken by fear. Let us choose our beliefs and live our truths... otherwise, this wilderness trap road will devour our dreams and our joy, and we will die here desolate in Exitville. Our potential left as a barren tomb. We have the *power* to choose our *beliefs*."

The words Peter hungered for were now present:

"Power."

"Choice."

The voice wasn't finished. "This wilderness road through Exitville is not going to define us but refine us!" the Growers shouted. "We choose to align our beliefs with the mission of team MPA. We will change the world we influence! Stay faithful to Coach, persevere through pain, and trust the process."

All Peter could do was stare at the gladiator arena in enlightened bewilderment. The gated passage wasn't stopped by a physical obstacle or barrier. The battle lines dividing the factions were their *beliefs*.

Someone cried again: "Old mindsets must die in the wilderness."

The arena shrunk as Peter sank into his seat. He was not alone. The dust in his lungs vanished, and fresh air blew in. Fear, self-doubt, and self-reliance wanted to kill his mindset and take out all MPAs.

The battle lines were drawn.

Perhaps his growth was in strengthening his belief muscles. If he held the power to choose what he believed, wouldn't this change his mindset? Wouldn't this shift his perspective? Surely, it would silence the voice of the Haters within.

Snapped back to reality, the war unfolded.

Despite the moving speech, many people remained stuck in Exitville, ignoring the voice of growth. The Haters' impenetrable mindsets overtaking them in the wilderness. Their ropes were laced with barbed wire.

The Growers united and charged forward through the wilderness trap. As joyous shouts trailed them, the confining ropes snapped like dry twigs.

Peter took one last look at the Haters. For some reason, he knew that this was his tipping point. Should he leave old tricks behind? Should he suffer in the wilderness trap? Should he exit MPA, blend in with the status quo, or press forward to embrace his growth potential?

He held the power of choice.

Peter stared through the soot on his windshield. His hand reached for the window washer lever – once, twice, three times – and the grime washed away. The loud ping brought him back to attention. Rubystar's warm voice came over the airwaves: "Peter, 'The *Power of Your Beliefs'* webinar starts in 15 minutes. Would you like to attend?"

Power of Beliefs Webinar

P eter's jaw dropped with the announcement of the *Power of Beliefs* webinar. He rushed to follow the trail blazed by the Growers out of Exitville before pulling into an empty parking lot. He plugged in his phone, which was drained to 3%. He chugged the last drop from his water bottle and opened the Rubystar app.

The virtual waiting room filled as Peter tapped his foot on the floorboard. Despite being stranded in Exitville, he'd never felt more connected.

Coach G led with a strong command voice that could awaken the dead, "Welcome, team MPA. It is *GrowthTime!* Are you ready to change the world you influence? I am thankful that you are committed to reaching your maximum potential. Let's focus on growing your life and leadership in pursuit of your higher purpose and pressing the mission of MPA forward!"

Peter pumped his fist, conforming to countless other MPAs on the webinar. Coach G's energy was infectious, his presence compelling, and each word hand-crafted. In just 30 seconds, Peter popped the glove compartment to find a pen and some paper.

His first note was a question:

What is my higher purpose?

Coach G continued, "As you know, today's webinar is on the Power of Beliefs. Everyone in attendance deals with different levels of adversity on their journey. No one is immune."

Everyone on camera nodded their heads in unison.

Coach G picked up the pace, "I have kept track of your progress. Rest assured, all roads must pass through Exitville for you to graduate MPA. This webinar is required as part of the second course. We will review your learnings, or shall I say 'growings'. Next, I will coach you on this topic, and then you will jump into your *GrowthTime!*

"The first part of this webinar is a self–reflection reality check. *What are you learning about yourself?* You have 10 minutes to answer the question. Write out all your thoughts and perceptions with no–holds–barred. Writing is winning in the game of clarity."

Peter tapped his pen on the wheel. *Writing is winning in the game of clarity* rang true as he echoed Coach G's words in his mind.

"Just be open and vulnerable," Coach G insisted. "Once you've finished, please send them through the messenger for review."

Peter relaxed and forced his foot to stop tapping the floorboard. With a deep exhale, the words flew off his pen:

> *My physical limitations, pain, lack of money, and fractured relationships hard-pressed me into a box that feels and looks restrictive. I am trapped, unable to break out. I know others face numerous trials, but I am wrestling with heartache and disappointment. Wondering why and how to move forward is a battle. The restlessness inside grows. Anxiety tries to overcome my being. Exasperation nestles into my being.*
>
> *From experience, I have learned that, despite obstacles and the emotions they bring, I have the power of choice inside my box. I can stay inside my box or climb out. I can choose my beliefs and how I respond.*
>
> *The tough truth I learned is my beliefs determine my actions, mental health, and well-being. I understand it is easy to be discouraged or offended. I return to a distorted Uville, a self-focused mindset, and get lost in internal grumbling and complaining. I become stuck.*
>
> *It is quite a battle to overcome. I need to grow my endurance muscles.*

Peter submitted his answer with more to write, yet almost out of time. His hand was shaking. His breathing accelerated, having just exposed himself to all.

Coach G jumped back on. "I appreciate all the transparent answers. What sticks out is that life is a contact sport," he said. "A battle rages, and we have choices in the war. Those choices decide not only if you win the war but also how you can overcome the journey of going through it."

"Here is the first coaching thought that will strengthen your battle. The power of choice is linked to your beliefs, the truths you embrace. Your *beliefs* will either *regress* your *progress*, keep you *stagnant*, or move you forward on your *quest* to be *great* in life."

Coach G flashed a PowerPoint slide:

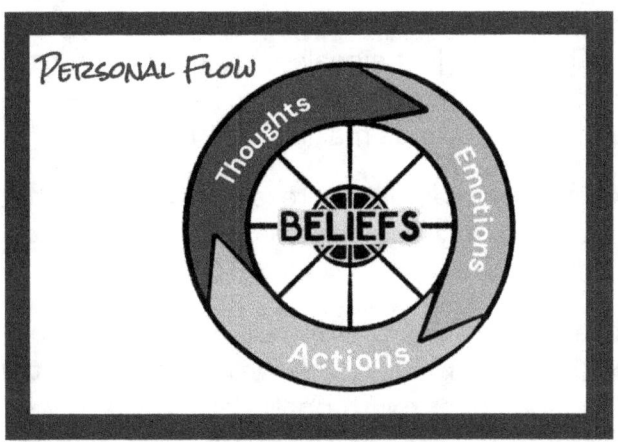

Coach G motioned to the viewers' section. "This diagram will help you become self-aware of how you operate. This model is called your *Personal Flow*. How you flow... you will go. Simple yet profound. Your beliefs are the center of the operation, let's call it your engine. Beliefs are your *chosen truths* about yourself, an experience, or a situation and directly influence how you navigate your life journey.

"Many of our beliefs are intrinsic and entwined into our subconscious being. They form based on your upbringing and experiences. They become ingrained and are arduous to change. Some adopted truths are good and empower your growth in life, while others limit your growth potential. Some will open the box of possibilities while others keep you locked up."

Coach G paused as many scribbled frantically. When they were finished, he smiled. "The mind is beautiful and complex. Thousands of thoughts and ideas come to us daily. They are the fuel for our engines, for better or worse." He motioned to his head and heart. "We filter our thoughts through our beliefs – truths. The stronger our beliefs, the less likely contrary, limiting, or negative thoughts will clog up our engines and impact our movement.

"Our thoughts, or mindsets, then stir up or trigger our emotions. Our emotions are the pistons in the engine. They are the catalysts that fire you into action. How you feel about a person, situation, or event will drive your behaviors and actions. Emotions aren't positive or negative; just signals allowing us to respond to life and its challenges. Strong emotions can be a beast to process, resolve and move towards making positive choices."

Coach paused again before expressing confidence to the team, "Now, don't worry. This webinar is recorded. All this coaching will be readily available."

"Our beliefs and truths are at the core of our actions. They are your operating system. The beliefs we hold onto, and the ones we let go of, decide your growth potential, growth of your mission, and most importantly, the state of your well-being."

Coach G paused a third time before offering, "I realize this is a lot to process, and you will need time to reflect. One thing to remember is that your actions or choices define you and your leadership. You are known and revealed to others by those actions."

Peter smiled from ear to ear, thankful for this weapon in the war. It was a good truth-bomb to learn the *Personal Flow* concept. He could see how the model would be a self-governor to process and check himself.

"The next question that will continue the growth journey is: 'What did you learn about operating beliefs from Exitville?' Take a few minutes to write out what resonated with you."

Peter hunched as he began to write...

I learned not to embrace limiting beliefs about myself or my situation despite fear and self-doubt pursuing me. These limiting beliefs consumed the Haters. To endure and overcome, I can't choose beliefs that restrict new outcomes, ones that lock me up and lead to discontentment and complaint. I am not helping anyone, including myself, in this state of being.

I notice I become inwardly restless, victim-centered, and resistant to hearing the voice of growth. Nothing good grows in this environment; weeds are choking me out. This gets me stuck in Exitville, just like the Haters.

*I am crowned by the mindset of the Growers – those who display quiet, still confidence. They choose **Faith** over **Fear**. To them, faith involves taking a risk and choosing to believe what is possible by moving past belief barriers rather than allowing fear of failure to cripple their journey.*

*The Growers combat their inner self-doubt by affirming **self-talk declarations** about themselves and their mission. They declared their desire for growth and allegiance to the higher purpose of team MPA.*

*It is clear that they operate through a belief system of **dependent-trust**. They surrender and trust in the bigger mission, each other, and leadership by breaking out of the box of self-reliance. They choose beliefs that don't limit outcomes or negatively impact their mental well-being. By embracing empowering truths, they are fueled by hope, even as they face crises head-on.*

That is what I want for my life.

Peter stopped writing as tears trickled down his cheeks.

"How are we all feeling?" Coach G prodded his webinar. "I believe it is time to wrap up our thoughts and share them in this safe space."

Peter turned off his camera to gather himself. In that moment of awareness, he noticed a direct message sent through the chat. It was Rubystar. His pupils grew as he read the request for Coach G to share his message.

His finger quivered as he clicked *"Yes."*

Peter's heart dropped. His last breath pressed through his trembling lungs, "That is what I want for my life," sent the chat messages crazy with affirmation.

Coach G smiled in admiration. "Thank you, Peter, for your honest and insightful learnings about the *Power of Beliefs*. You expressed the fundamental operating beliefs well. I know many here tonight feel you and desire the same thing. The coaching moment I hope resonates with you is two foundational truths that will guide your growth in the battle."

Coach G flashed the first slide on the screen.

Limiting beliefs restrict your potential outcomes

They are the enemy in the battle

Then, the second slide.

> ***Empowering beliefs unlock growth opportunities and open limitless possibilities***
>
> ***They are your allies in the battle***

After highlighting some key points, Coach shifted gears in anticipation of finalizing the session. "Now, the last question of the night for you to self-reflect and answer is: 'What are your options going forward?' Please write them out."

Peter's steel eyes glared out of the once grime-infested window. Exitville was a microcosm of his struggle. The wilderness was a paradigm box. Staying in the box presented veiled control of his life. It was full of resentment, and Peter had no room to breathe. Breaking out took courage – a courage that was rising within.

Three clear options locked in:

1. Go back to his old mindset of self-focus, Uville

2. Drop out of MPA and stay stuck in mediocrity

3. Choose his ally of empowering beliefs and move forward

Coach G glowed like a proud father. "You did amazing tonight, team MPA," he said. "This coaching space allows you to explore options without discounting any. Options create possibilities. All are practical choices – no right or wrong ones, but options. Just let the voice of wisdom speak to you. Just before we wrap up, please check your inbox as I have sent additional *GrowthTime!* tools," Coach G rallied his MPAs.

As Peter scrolled to his messages, he reclined. He lifted his gaze and peered through the glass T-top panel to admire the sparkles of the heavens.

MY GROWTHTIME!

COACH Q

Let's get some dust out of your lungs, Windex the windshield, and overcome the wilderness trap. Unlocking the clear victory path begins with two words:

1. Exposure

2. Vulnerability

You can't fight a war without bringing the dark into the light. Limiting beliefs can be dealt with when you are willing to expose their exact nature and the restrictive box they create – shining the light on how they are locking down powerful potentials and fresh outcomes.

The most common belief barriers must be exposed:

FEAR:

I am afraid of failing. I am afraid of having no money. I am afraid of being alone.

SELF–DOUBT:

I am doubting my ability to perform. I feel like an impostor. I can't do that because.

SELF–RELIANCE:

I must figure this out by myself. I will not trust anyone. I am in full control.

Vulnerability is a willingness to expose these truths – to yourself, another human being, and the Divine himself. The result of vulnerability is breaking the enemy's power that is locking you up. New options will become available to you. The power to choose to operate by faith, with self-affirming declarations and dependent-trust will break through all belief barriers... and joy will be your reward.

SELF-ASSESSMENT

Break out your *GrowthTime!* journal and create space to assess your story with the following questions. Go deep into vulnerability and exposure.

- Where have limiting belief barriers immobilized you?
    - Dreams
    - Relationships
    - Finances
    - Career
    - Life experiences
    - Goals
    - Personal growth

- When have you been successful in operating with empowering beliefs?
    - Faith
    - Self-talk declarations
    - Dependent-trust

GROWTHTIME

Let's practice the *Personal Flow*:

1. What is the biggest obstacle/challenge you are dealing with?

2. What are your beliefs about yourself or the situation?

3. Write out common thoughts or the story you keep telling yourself.

4. Describe in detail the emotions that come forth.

5. What actions or non-action have you taken?

The next step is exposing the nature of the beliefs operating within you:

What fears are attached to this challenge?

What negative self-talk is showing up?

Where is self-reliance winning?

Actions to win the war:

- Record the steps of faith you will take to overcome this fear

- Write out three specific affirmations that oppose the limiting belief lies and declare them for the next seven days

- Commit to paper how you will operate in dependent-trust

ENCOURAGEMENT

Follow Peter's lead. After you have completed the growth work, share your response with another person. Your growth is tied to how vulnerable you choose to be. Give them your accountable actions and a timeline for completing them. *Be strong and courageous. It's your time to break through belief barriers to unlock your best life!*

Additional resources are available at mygrowthtime.com.

THE POWER OF PERSONAL LIBERTY

The Higher Purpose

Peter's eyes scanned the empty parking lot as a PDF named "Limiting Beliefs" downloaded to his phone. Chills ran down his arms as he reflected on the boarded-up, abandoned commercial buildings, smashed windows, graffiti-splashed concrete, and weeds sprouting through the asphalt.

Life's unforgiving demons hovered around each corner, just waiting to steal someone's purpose or, even worse, destroy their potential. No remorse, just robbing joy and crucifying hope.

Countless dreams lay abandoned on the concrete prison of Exitville. Countless souls relegated to misery. The war of beliefs was real. The casualties were endless.

Something had to be done.

Coach G's voice interrupted Peter's awakened sorrow, "Thank you for jumping into your *GrowthTime!* The choice is yours. The clear path has been revealed. I am pulling for each of you to defeat your enemy."

Peter shifted in his seat.

"As your Coach," Coach G said, "I challenge you to overcome this wilderness trap. Support is always available. Thank you for showing up tonight and keep pursuing your higher purpose."

Peter's mind paced back and forth. There was the question again...

What is my higher purpose?

The moment arrived as his eyes fixated on the blue sky. The simple, profound depth of the MPA's vision to change the world he influenced. That was *his* higher purpose.

The image of Jhonny greeting him in Uville flashed through his mind. He envisioned being an ambassador like Jhonny. He would share the message of the *Power of U!* and wear a purple heart to revive those dying on the battlefield of their beliefs. If basketball was fixed in his review mirror, he could be at peace with finding his greater purpose in life – a purpose that transcended what he did.

Electricity flowed through Peter. The belief locked in; his thoughts fueled the fire, and his emotions sparked Peter into action. It was a pure *Personal Flow*. He quickly capitalized on his self-declaration:

> *Coach G,*
>
> *First, I want to apologize for disconnecting over the last several months. It has been quite the battle to keep sanity within my crumbling world. I am reaffirming and declaring my commitment to team MPA. With the lessons I have learned, I commit myself to impacting this world one person at a time. The people in my path of life will be those I will influence and inspire. I will live a life of empowering beliefs and win this war. I will follow the clear path of the Growers, stay committed to my personal growth, and help others do the same.*
>
> *It's my GrowthTime!,*
>
> *Peter*

He proudly hit the send button and then tapped the ignition starter. The Camaro roared like a lion once more...

The cautionary cones and flashing warning lights disappeared. The deserted single-lane road returned to a two-way highway. Rubystar helped navigate a few turns before arriving back in familiar territory. And just as he unfolded his long legs to get out of the car, another *ping!* It was from Coach G.

I am proud of you!

Coach G, Sent 4:54 p.m.

You will be a leader of leaders.

Coach G, Sent 4:54 p.m.

It was the affirmation a boy longed to hear from his dad. A voice pushing him to stand firm in the face of contrary winds. His shoulders pulled back. His head tilted forward as he strolled towards the physical therapist's front door.

His war flag had arisen.

Despite the circumstances, Peter had a refreshed love affair with the voice of growth. Unfortunately, the unclear voice of the doctors wouldn't relent. They didn't have answers on how to treat his deteriorating back. His body wasn't responding to therapy, manipulations, or injections. Further tests confirmed his spine's regression.

Yet, Peter chose to take a position of power in the war. Looking past the battle-torn horizon, he said, "Not this time. I refuse to lose my joy. I know the truth of exercising empowering beliefs. No barrier will crush my beliefs."

He envisioned a ginormous wall as he leaned into dependent-trust in the Divine's sovereign plan – the wall between him and destiny. Peter was learning that he had to throw his beliefs at the barriers to break through. There was no way around it, no way over it. He had to go through it. Throw after throw after throw he hurled them at the wall.

Two years in and not a chink in the wall. Peter was fulfilled by staying true to his higher purpose. He used every opportunity to share the message of MPA with technicians, therapists, friends, and anyone in his path. People marveled at his contagious joy in the face of adversity, bringing a profound sense of satisfaction to his growing endurance muscles.

It was a sudden shift that ruptured his newfound steadfast approach to the mundane. It came on a typical scorching July day. After an intense physical therapy session, he dropped his bag by the laundry, grabbed lunch and two ice packs before heading to the couch. He then clicked on his AirPods to download some Jhonnyisms. A deep sleep overcame Peter.

In his surreal slumber, a near-death experience of bright light enveloped him. He heard air pressure compressed as through an expanding balloon. It expanded into his degenerated, decayed lower spine. The air was warm – transcendent – soothing to dead disks.

Undeniable. Palatable.

He turned around, only to see the slow-motion fade of a hand moving away from his back. Peter's eyes popped open. His frame projected off the couch, landing with an earth-quaking thud. Knees on the carpet, arms lifted high, mouth open in bewilderment.

As sweat glistened off his forehead, he panted and thought: *Did that happen… really happen?*

He twisted left. Twisted right. No snap, crackle or pop. Touched his toes. No shooting streaks down his legs. In adulation, he reached for the largest object he could find. He yanked the plug from the wall of the outdated 55-inch television and began to pace the apartment hallway.

No pain.

Was this real? Had that hand been the surgeon? He dropped the TV against the wall, split open the front door and took off barefoot. He flew down two flights of stairs before launching into a game-day sprint down the street.

He pulled up several hundred yards from the neighborhood stop sign, closed his eyes, and waited, counting: *"8, 9, 10."*

All the pain was gone.

The doctors marveled, and his family rejoiced. No rational explanation existed for the radical reversal of fortune, just praise for the Divine restoration. Peter marinated in gratitude, knowing this supernatural encounter was a sign. He set his social media ablaze, sharing the powerful news. God had granted him a fresh lease on life.

Peter was starved for movement. He took off to find a new path for meaningful income to erase the financial burden. With the faith engine roaring like a lion, he focused on the health and fitness industry. Years of fighting through physical therapy awakened a deep compassion to help those struggling. Combined with his background and a zest for exercise and nutrition, it looked like a golden door swung open to join FitLife.

FitLife was a regional brand of elite fitness centers that was well on its way to establishing itself as the biggest and brightest brand in the fitness space. Peter snatched up the role of Fitness Sales Coach. The opportunity looked promising and came with ample room for upward growth, and he was drawn to their compelling mission:

Changing Lives with Fitness

His job was on the front lines, selling and promoting the fitness gospel. It was an easy sell for Peter because he strongly believed everyone needed fitness. For him, being healthy and fit was part of reaching one's full potential. Most wrestled to make fitness a way of life. Doubt, self–limiting beliefs, personal hardships, and excuses all littered the battlefield. Helping people say, "Yes" to fitness was victory and a means to fulfilling his higher purpose.

Peter found his groove using persuasive conversation skills to influence people over the coming years. He discovered his talent for helping people work through emotional and mental barriers. Focusing on one customer at a time, just as he had promised Coach G, he embraced his gift. Peter called this the "loving-the-one-you-are-with" sales approach. Understanding his customers' needs, goals, and desires was instrumental to his success. This consultative, relationship-based approach worked like fire touching gasoline... explosive!

The accolades, awards, and contest-winning trips overtook his mantle as he secured the seat as FitLife's top sales leader just six months into his role.

One client, Kayla, stood out as the reason Peter loved working for FitLife. She came in distressed. Her shoulders hung low and her eyes were glossy. Peter pushed his lunch aside and left his desk to talk with Kayla. He asked her, "What motivates you to seek a change, Kayla?"

It turned out Kayla had lost her teenage son in an accident. Mired in depression and grief, this was her brave attempt for help. Peter's heart filled with compassion.

After nearly two hours of offering support, Peter rejoiced when Kayla decided to start a new fitness plan. Day by day, she showed up. Each day brought a bigger smile, a lighter heart, and a bounce to her step. Peter often gave her a high-five at her 10 a.m. arrival, inspired by the jumbled puzzle pieces of her life coming together.

Stories like these earned Peter the Life-Changer Award, recognizing team members who go above and beyond. The recognition marked another step forward in embodying the MPA vision... and paved the way for growth.

The pace was electric as Peter progressed from Fitness Sales Coach to Assistant Manager to Sales Manager. He was soon entrusted with driving sales for the area's premier location. A noted high-flyer, he was validated for his positive approach and ability to influence calling card performances.

As time wore on, Peter entered a sweet zone of continuous growth. He skillfully cultivated his small team of Fitness Sales Coaches. Trent stood out, shoulders above his proteges – a young buck from a broken home living far away. Driven, a quick thinker, and an uber-talented player, he had a sharp edge – ready to cut when pushed against.

Peter saw himself in Trent and felt the haunt of a young man leaving his driveway years ago with a Boulder-sized chip of resentment. On lunch breaks, workouts, and long coffee breaks, Peter shared the life lessons of Uville and Exitville. During their working hours, he poured into developing his sales skills. Trent soaked in the relationship and was promoted up the ranks.

It was a victorious day when Trent joined MPA.

Peter stayed faithful to the MPA community and thrived with the most recent change: app updates. These included personal profiles with interests, values, and stories. The new app's interface made it unique and easy to meet other like-minded MPAs. Peter found encouragement in sending words of support to his fellow MPAs, and he appreciated the reciprocated love. He actively posted, shared, and received valuable mindset tips on the community thread.

Peter slept in peace, evergreen-glad to have moved past the tribulations of Exitville. The wilderness a distant image in his rearview mirror. The road expanded ahead.

The Perfect Storm

Life blew a beautiful kiss during his ascent in FitLife. A son was welcomed into Peter's world. Reggie glued him and Shannell together. The boy was his first-round pick, a homerun hitter destined for impact.

Peter vowed that Reggie's upbringing would be different. He intended to bring love, joy, and adventure into his son's life. Peter already had the future mapped out – coaching sports, summer days at the beach, trips to the park, slip-sliding in the rain, teaching him lessons of MPA...

The endless list of possibilities.

Yet, in the first 72 hours, Peter came to terms with sacrificing stretches of service. Rotating midnight feedings, changing diapers, driving around to soothe colic episodes, and even washing his clothes stained with baby formula.

As days passed into months, Peter found fatherhood glorious. In his professional life he was also basking in the growth of his FitLife career. And that speedy Camaro was turned in for a minivan. Oddly enough, the car dealer marveled at the interior's mint condition at trade-in time. With nothing to hide, all those rips and tears had mended up.

After four years of service in FitLife, Peter noticed a light rain beginning to fall. The sun slipped behind the clouds, slicking the roads. Dark clouds hovered on the horizon.

All was not well in the FitLife world.

Performance was praised over ethical principles. Many high-flyers remained employed despite breaking the Code of Conduct policy. Customer service took a backseat to sales as increasing profit was more important than the needs of those who paid the bills.

The organization's accountability flow didn't empower management to address day-to-day operational issues. Four chefs couldn't exist in the kitchen debating the menu. Leadership shifted and changed direction, goals, and objectives, confusing everyone. Work hours and expectations stretched despite brewing employee labor lawsuits starting to make headline news.

Peter couldn't continue ignoring the writing on the wall.

The contradicting expectations and rewards gave Peter countless restless nights. Although the core vision was significant, the disregard for values turned him over, churning... again and again, as the company promise of change never arrived.

A bolt of blue destroyed any lingering loyalty Peter felt toward FitLife. Hypocrisy unplugged by misleading team members, including himself, with their pay structure. His compensation plan was changed four times within six months, often with a few days' notice. Peter concluded that messing with a man's money was no light matter, as each change promised increased rewards and delivered lower returns.

The turnover of team members was like a revolving door: recruit, hire, train... and depart. Peter's trust in leadership hard nosedived. All the stirred-up muck created long dinnertime conversations with Shannell who, he noticed, was becoming more and more withdrawn. Perhaps if he worked harder, she would go back to being the Shannell he once knew.

And then Peter met Craig.

Craig was a self-professed MPA, a fellow churchgoer Peter met while at the park with their kids. They hit it off. Craig was affable and had an uncanny charm that could sell life insurance to the deceased. A clean-shaven head with a light scuffle gray splashed beard, he was always dressed to impress.

Craig had launched a marketing business venture for owner-operated fitness centers. He offered Peter a partnership opportunity to drive sales for the new start-up.

Perhaps this was his next growth step into the entrepreneurial space – a tantalizing idea to elevate his creative, adventurous desires and build something from scratch. He eagerly welcomed a fresh start beyond his current role, ready to move on from a company he had outgrown. He just didn't know if this was it.

With the sour rain not relenting at FitLife, Peter's itch to blaze a new path kept gaining momentum. Perhaps it was premature of him to so willingly believe in Craig, but it was a necessary distraction from the failing aspects of FitLife.

A few more rounds of late-night conversations added dashes of premature grey to his head. And yet, his mornings leaning into Divine guidance kept tipping the scale to making a break for it. The decisive nudge came through a message hand-crafted by Jhonny.

Peter would have scrolled past the thread without catching a glimpse of Jhonny's smile. He scrolled up as the man himself was saying:

> *Changing the world requires the brave to move out into deep waters. Courage comes in the face of the storm. The storms in life present the biggest opportunities. The opportunity to reach your potential. This comes by getting out of the boat of comfortability.*

The message fell on good ears. Peter joined forces with Craig. Drafting, revising, and printing his resignation gave him shaky hands and a racing heart, but it was necessary. Jhonny's words were what Peter needed. So, he made a graceful exit from FitLife on a refreshing fall day filled with mixed emotions of sadness... and pure adrenaline.

One chapter closed, and another was beginning.

Peter hit the pavement running with a full-speed sales engine. The slick roads were drying up. He was jiving with Craig, the majority partner... and promising results were in the forecast.

Peter's perception was dead wrong.

The sun was setting on an early spring day. Peter had hurried home with a pep in his step. He grinned just thinking about surprising Shannell with a night out to their favorite spot. He sprinted up the apartment stairs only...

Shannell was already standing at the door. He thought she was there to greet him again, to welcome him back with loving arms.

"Shannell, I've been so..." Peter started, ready to cherish their moment together.

His eyes landed on the suitcase at her feet. Confidence slipping away, Shannell, in a steel-fisted frame of mind, bee-lined past him. A painful ghost of her yesteryear returned to haunt her, and she couldn't stand a moment longer within her skin. He had seen the signs: contentious, angry, unaccountable, ever since she had drifted away from MPA in the wilderness season. Every approach he had tried only seemed to push her farther away, down a spiraling dark path.

He never thought it would come to this. She snatched Reggie under her wing and hurled disillusioned accusations at Peter.

"Shannell, you know it's not true," Peter begged.

"Are you calling me a liar?"

"I am saying that you need help, and I want to help you. Don't... don't do this."

Peter gasped for breath, wondering how this monster reared its ugly head. Before he could catch his breath, Shannell bulldozed down the stairs steaming to the carport. She never looked back despite his begging and pleading for reasonability.

She was gone... and Peter was alone. The dream of his life transformed into an emotional nightmare. The road ahead washed out.

Without Shannell or Reggie, a respite to the beach became Peter's nightly solace. He often wandered along the shore, where the crashing waves met the wind, bracing himself against the tide, knees buckled... imprints in the sand. His voice echoed over the waves as deep prayer became his confidant. Night after night, pleading for Shannell's sanity to be restored.

The work demands didn't let up. It was a tightrope walk of daily interruptions from the ever-present conflicts, with texts, calls, accusations, and misunderstandings overwhelming his capacity. It took all his fighting just to show up and perform his job. He just wasn't ready to throw in the towel. Surely, wholeness of mind could be restored... couldn't it?

Peter didn't know quit. He had broken through walls before. This was just a different wall that required a bigger rock of dependent-trust to throw at it. Surely a breakthrough could happen again?

Peter crawled forward, pressing day by day, moment by moment. He understood well that you only get one shot to blow, one lifetime. Though his struggles felt deeply personal, he knew they weren't unique. He had witnessed tragic scenarios unfold before with clients and team members.

Personal relationships caused pain – deep emotional pain. And yet, the clock of life and professional responsibility paid no attention.

Peter still had to show up, somehow. Even with the dull ache of misery, he gave it his best shot to find some semblance of peace once more. He doubled down on old habits and explored new ones to create order: diverging versions of meditation, exercise, counsel, prayer, and daily MPA podcasts.

Then... *Boom!* It was the sound of thunder threatening to end his story.

It was Craig.

His character revealed massive cracks. There was a twitch in his confident flow, which Peter spotted when he asked for proof of sales. Craig shifted the subject and avoided following through on looping him in. Peter asked for support in the sales process, only to be let down thrice. Commitments were made but then directions switched.

Peter was confronted with the same theme but a different variation. People saying one thing and doing another. Peter coined the term: "hypocrite monster" – the beast who lives within. The inherent creature contradicting values.

This monster was overtaking Craig.

Peter continued his work alone and expanded the sales funnel. As revenue increased, Craig's monster increased. He fell behind on his commitments and blamed others. He also stayed off work and was caught lying about meetings, results, and even to the customers.

After one year, Craig swallowed the cash and vanished.

Peter wrestled for clarity, grappling with what felt like needless, merciless pain. A pain inflicted by the hypocritical monster living unchecked within humanity. Many nights he rocked his favorite lazy boy chair trying to make sense of the madness. What was the solution? How could he help someone else before the monster claimed its rights?

The moon illuminated the night as questions surfaced from the deep:

1. *How can you still **show up** as a professional when storms invade your world?*

2. *Why does the hypocrite monster overtake value-spoken people?*

Peter Arrives in Showville

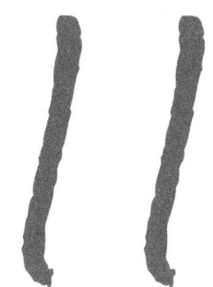

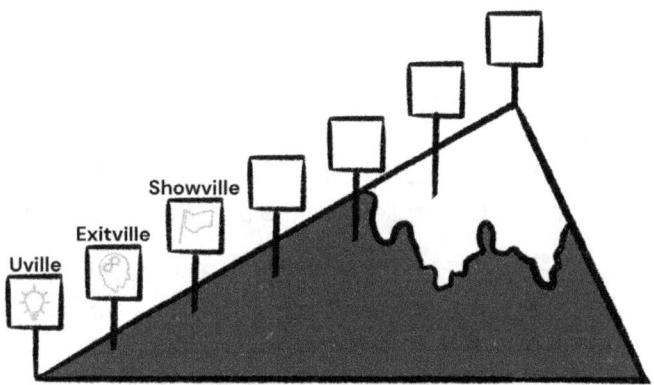

"Head down, focus on the road ahead," Peter sang as the tune echoed through his minivan, rain pelting his windshield. The wipers squeaked as the car crawled through the monsoon-like conditions. There was no detour sign ahead; there were bumps, potholes, and washed-out roads.

The storm took Peter for a ride. It was an expedition he never expected.

Through the downpour, a Vegas-style light flashed across his eyes. He had arrived in Showville. It was a glitzy town lit up like a Christmas tree, with neon lights, flickering signs, and streets buzzing with anticipation.

This must be the place where stars hang out, he mused.

Peter could barely hold his head up. His shirt was sweaty, his eyes bloodshot... and his stomach growled like a stray cat. Looking to refuel, he pulled into the parking lot of a local restaurant called Mr. Good Burgers. The effervescent sign with a cowboy lassoing an oversized burger called his name. He hoped the moniker didn't find favor with the hypocrite monster:

The Best Burger and Service in Showville

Peter found a spot in the crowded parking lot. A quick once-over lightened his load as the van somehow made it through. He grabbed his weathered Shippers baseball cap and dashed through the downpour, splashing through puddles before ducking inside.

The counters shined, the floor glistened, and the cowboy-themed decor was immaculate. Someone loved this place. Everything appeared in order, spit-shined, and tooth-brushed clean. His shoulders relaxed; a smile cracked as he approached the check-in.

The host greeted him. "Hi, I am Ms. Kelly. Welcome to the best burger and service in Showville! Thank you for coming in. How is your day going?" she inquired.

It was the inviting smile and cordial disposition that brought hope to Peter. Her tone, body language, and words released the tension that had recoiled his body. She had a firm-pressed uniform with a bright orange polo shirt. Her shiny name badge drew his attention. It said:

Peter played the honest card, "Pretty tapped out, Ms. Kelly, but looking forward to some good eats. I'm a first-timer. Just need a table for one. Thank you."

Ms. Kelly grabbed a menu and led him to a cozy booth. She offered a complimentary basket of garlic mini fries, which he accepted. After explaining an overview of tonight's special, she let him know his server, Mr. James, would be with him momentarily.

Peter sank into the booth. *This is off to a good start*, he thought. Ms. Kelly certainly lived up to her unique name badge.

Peeking up, Peter noticed a family of five across from him. There was a bouquet and a ginormous award plaque at the center of the table. Not trying to eavesdrop, the conversation floated his way. He could hear grumblings from the teenage kids.

"Dude, where is our food? What is Mr. Brandon doing?"

"We have been waiting 30 minutes."

"How long does it take to get a refill?"

"I have not seen our server in 10 minutes."

One of the girls even remarked, "I think our server is kinda rude. He acts like we're an inconvenience. He keeps saying it is not his fault but the cooks'. Like we care? He needs to go back to the Showville School of Training."

The mother shook her head in disgusted agreement. Peter could feel the mounting tension as he eyed the father's clenched jaw, about to crack his enamel. "This was supposed to be a family night to honor your volleyball championship," he seethed to his daughter.

The celebratory night was now stress night at Mr. Good Burgers.

Peter decided to scroll through his phone. The mention of a "School of Training" piqued his curiosity. Perhaps he could find something on Google.

However, he didn't get very far as Mr. James arrived in a New York minute. He had kind eyes and soft features as he effortlessly initiated small talk. His genuine approach alleviated any anxiety from the nearby table. The "Mr. Juicy Deluxe with fried pickles" recommendation seemed a winner. He noted Peter's fixings and confirmed his order before grabbing a peach lemonade. Peter took notice of his name badge as well. It said:

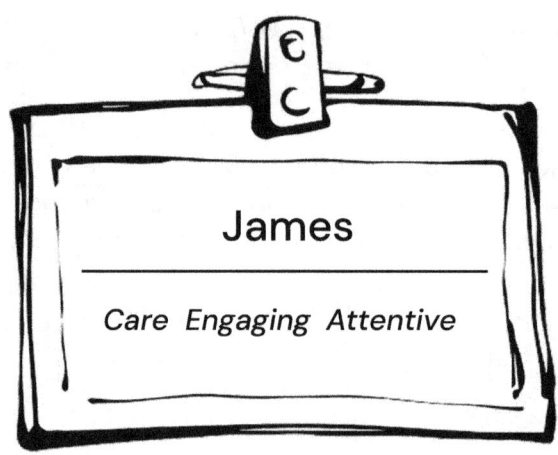

As Peter annihilated the garlic fries, his attention was pulled to the waiter who arrived with the family's food. His eye contact was non-existent, countenance downcast, and speech muffled. Not to mention, his shirt was untucked, and he kept doing an awkward hair-flop routine.

Peter chewed another fry just as Mr. Brandon's hand slipped on the double-stacked plates. Mr. Juicy Burger splattered firmly on the mother's lap.

The tipping point arrived.

The father's face squinched with fire as fumes blew from his ears. Mr. Brandon didn't miss a beat. One more hair flop before apologizing, "The cook didn't wipe dry the rim of the plates." But the father's patience was ice under a desert sun.

"I want the manager!" he demanded.

Peter's experience meter slid down his lemonade's straw. The scene robbed him of the peaceful enjoyment Mr. Good Burger promised. He pushed aside his fries, having lost his appetite.

Mr. Brandon shook his head, taking the walk of shame to find his manager. It was then that Peter caught a glimpse of his badge:

Brandon

Excellence Fun Ownership

Peter scratched his head, reflecting on the cataclysmic breakdown. *How fitting*, Mr. Brandon's actions violated his clever name badge. Intentions lost in translation. Words, but not deliverables. It reminded Peter of the reruns he had witnessed in his own life. FitLife leaders, Craig, Shannell.... all he could hear were the celebratory shouts of that vicious hypocrite monster. Another victim.

The manager was apologetic as Peter overheard his sincere, empathetic approach. It was customer service clean-up time, and to his credit, he lowered the barometer of fury. After restoring tranquility, the manager darted towards Peter's booth. Peter zoomed in on his badge:

General Manager
Mr. Isaiah

Integrity Service Responsibility

Peter saw the meekness in Mr. Isaiah's eyes as he broached. "I sincerely apologize for tonight's service experience. Clearly, we did not deliver on our service promise. Tonight's bill is on us. Here is also a gift card for a second chance. Again, I am sorry about your experience tonight. Is there anything else I can do?"

Having walked this tightrope with his sales team, Peter knew the manager's pain. Peter took the high road and commended Mr. Isaiah for navigating the evening's adventure. "No, thank you, but I appreciate the gesture. My waiter has been phenomenal. The food is amazing. I will say I appreciated watching your customer service approach. Mistakes happen, and sometimes it is just near-impossible to get good help."

Mr. Isaiah bowed. "It is on me. I take responsibility. The waiter did not graduate from the Showville School of Training and I put him on the serving floor. I should have paid more attention to the signs."

Peter raised a brow. "What do you mean by the Showville School of Training? What happens there?"

"Ah, you must be a visitor to town,'" Mr. Isaiah said. "Well, here in Showville, we offer this course that teaches people how to self-manage themselves to success."

"That sounds like an intriguing course. How does it work?" Peter asked.

"The quick version teaches people to not just physically show up for work but learn how to show up the best authentic version of themselves. They learn effective self-care habits that help them overcome themselves and life challenges. Have you noticed their name tags?"

Peter responded, "Yes, I thought it quite clever to identify themselves with adjectives they value. Unless, of course, you don't live up to them."

"Agreed," Mr. Isaiah said. "They define their values and what others can expect from them. We hire people who match our value system. The challenge is not all people deliver on their brand promise. The Showville school helps them to avoid life's roller coaster. Sometimes up. Sometimes down. Sometimes caught in a loop."

"Yep, the hypocrite monster takes over and keeps people on that roller coaster." Peter replied.

Mr. Isaiah chuckled. "Yes, that is a term I haven't heard before, but I will use it in my coaching. Well, I apologize again, and I hope you enjoy the rest of your visit to Showville. Please come back and see us again."

Peter thanked Mr. Isaiah for living up to his values and standing up for Mr. Good Burger's promise. He devoured the best burger in Showville. With the last bite secured in his belly, Peter left an oversized tip for Mr. James and headed out.

The storm had come to a quiet end. The drops glistened with glee on his front hood. He was optimistic that the voice of growth was coming his way. The issue was clear: He just needed resources like this Showville School.

Yet, how could one better self-manage themselves to success? There just had to be a clear path to take.

Peter left Showville and returned to his empty apartment. Unable to fully comprehend it, he needed guidance. So, he booked a one-on-one coaching session with MPA, hoping it would help him dig deeper and find clarity. Who knew, perhaps MPA offered a course comparable to this Showville School of Training?

A sorrowful silence descended as Peter turned the key and nudged the door open. It was dark and empty, an abyss without the patter of Reggie's feet and his little arms wrapping around Peter's legs as he came home from work.

Eyes burning, Peter threw his hoodie on the table and collapsed onto his oversized couch. He picked his head up just long enough to book his coaching session before drifting off.

Coached Up!

Peter awoke energized. He sprung from the couch, took a hot shower, and was thankful for the aftertaste of Mr. Good Burger's garlic fries still on his lips. Sunday service, housekeeping, and weekly meal preparation were next on his to-do list. He scheduled his workout sessions and circled Monday at 5 p.m. with five stars. His coaching session had been confirmed, and to his delight, it was with Jhonny.

Peter was chomping at the bit for 5 p.m. to arrive. He had already submitted the pre-coaching questionnaire, which asked about his current experience, expectations, and what he hoped to gain from the coaching session. The coaching platform to log into was Vision, a 3D virtual video conference room pioneered by MPA. It put the participants together in a real-life-like setting using advanced virtual imaging technology.

Peter sat at his kitchen table with a pen and some paper. The session opened with him and Jhonny sitting on the beach in lounge chairs. Peter exhaled. The beach was his haven, a place to refresh, and he assumed Jhonny had taken the time to read his profile.

Jhonny's voice lifted Peter's spirits. He kicked off the conversation by expressing his admiration for Peter – his resolve, tenacity, and evolving desire for the voice of growth. This call out of his character endured Peter even more. Someone had recognized his efforts.

Knowing he was tracking well to graduate from the MPA felt good. "Just wanted to say I am honored to be a part of team MPA," Peter said. "It has been quite the ride since we met in Uville. I had no idea how deep I was lost in the matrix. You pulled me out. Thanks for the love."

Peter was *honored* that Jhonny was his coach today. Although he was Coach G's son, he did not carry arrogance or entitlement. He worked tirelessly to connect with each MPA team member and express Coach G's philosophy. Jhonny was the MVP of MPA: a living legend showing an exemplary way for others to follow. It was impossible to fathom Jhonny's impact on countless lives in the program. He fiercely championed the mission that every person could change the world they influenced.

Coach G was the leader, but having someone like Jhonny with boots on the ground was priceless.

"Well, I am thrilled you reached out and scheduled this coaching session," said Jhonny. "Glad you put the Pride-Ego aside and didn't allow self-reliance to win the battle. I read your responses and want to clarify that your goal at the end of this session is to understand better how to self-manage yourself to success and have practical application tips?" Jhonny asked.

"Yes, that is my primary goal, but any insight into how to help others past this hypocrite monster would be welcomed too," Peter said.

"Sounds good. I like that term: hypocrite monster. Isn't that the truth? Please realize we will coach you down an exploratory path to find answers. Hopefully, I can offer insight on the places you get stuck... even be a guide to clarity."

Jhonny nodded, "Coaching starts with understanding your perspective. What is your current reality? We can move forward from there."

"Well, I am hungry to reach my potential and be successful, but I keep getting my donkey kicked. The lessons from the *Power of U!* and the *Power of Beliefs* keep me sane. Yet, life's roller coaster moments affect how I show up. I admit it... I am angry underneath it all. Feeling betrayed and disappointed." Peter paused as his eyebrows furrowed.

"Too much unnecessary pain. And recently, I visited Showville, which highlighted my underlying gripe," Peter said.

Jhonny held his attentive coaching space as his heart grieved. Watching MPAs stumble and crumble only heightened his urgency to empower people to overcome themselves. "OK, Peter, I am familiar with Showville as other MPAs have visited that town. Let's start there. What did you learn from your time there?"

Peter sat up. The vein on his neck bulged through his collar, and his Italian roots caused his hands to flare violently. "Some people are horrific at living out their values. A sub-zero standard. Misguided jerks who create pain. It's like they love the power of the hypocrite monster, enjoying when it goes beast-mode."

Peter paused... but wasn't done. "They are a waterless well – a walking contradiction. What is unfathomable and gut-wrenching is how much potential is wasted and the following senseless drama. The craziness... what would be possible if people were trained to show up? Things could be different. All things would be possible, right?"

Jhonny appreciated the candid, fervent response. "I hear the emotional frustration and can see the angst in your expressions. I also hear a genuine hope for a better tomorrow for others."

"Yeah, I hear and feel that too." Peter paused in reflection.

"I'm curious: what are some ways you currently live out your values? And perhaps explore how do you currently self-manage?"

Peter stopped in his tracks, having only partially explored that path. "Hmm, I guess I don't really have a solid answer. I try to focus on positive things. I often exercise — although that has been slipping until recently. I have tried to meditate, but that feels awkward. I listen to all MPA's daily encouragements. God also helps... I probably could lean more heavily into that now that I think of it."

"It sounds like you have some good thoughts but not a clear path or strongly defined habits to build upon," Jhonny said.

"That's spot on."

"Okay, well, I can give you a coaching perspective on what has worked for other MPAs. Then, let me know what resonates with you. We can explore some next-step options and then get into action. Sound good?"

"That sounds amazing," Peter replied, feeling comfortable and safe in this exploratory coaching space.

"Let's start by acknowledging the hypocrite monster you mentioned as the unavoidable part of the human experience. Getting free from this monster starts with knowledge of self. You cannot manage what you do not intimately know. Understand that as Showville has a school to train people, so does MPA. It is an online group training program that teaches you the fundamentals of self-mastering and the *Power of your Personal Liberty*," Jhonny elaborated.

Peter was confused. "Wait, what the heck is personal liberty? And what does that have to do with showing up or managing yourself to success?"

"Great question. Your personal *liberty* is your internal *freedom* meter. A freedom that allows you to live out your values without contradiction. A freedom that allows you to show up for the people you love and lead. It allows for your true authentic self to live and the best God-version of you to manifest — keeping that hypocrite monster locked away."

Peter locked in on every word that dripped out.

"This freedom empowers you to process daily challenges without getting crushed. It clears the internal mind clutter and heavy heart weights pulling you down. When you learn to self-master yourself, you will *expedite your life and leadership growth*. Then you can level up in your mission to change the world you influence," Jhonny replied.

"Ok, that is a unique perspective," Peter quipped. "Yet it makes sense. The more internal mind clutter and heavy heart I have carried, the harder it is to be present at the moment and be authentic to my values. So, how do you grow your personal liberty?" Peter asked.

"Simple, yet difficult," said Jhonny. "It starts with truth. Embracing and applying truth increases your freedom. As Coach G has ingrained in our culture, the truth will set you free."

"Would you like to continue to coach down this path?" Jhonny paused to ask.

"Yes, definitely," Peter affirmed.

"Let's start simple," Jhonny continued.

"My experience in coaching is adversity attacks your inner peace. Without resolving or releasing the stress, your well-being is compromised. Over time, we begin to follow the path of least resistance, letting the inner monster slowly take control. The result is that you do what you don't want to do – go against your values or words. How does this click with you?" Jhonny asked.

"Quite a bit. I am having an 'ah-ha' clarity moment. The part that isn't as clear is how to connect growing my liberty to self-managing me. You mentioned this concept of knowledge of self. It's a fuzzy path right now."

"Are you open to me showing a coaching tool?" Jhonny asked.

"Yes, please," Peter exuberantly answered.

Jhonny flashed an image as Peter leaned in. "Knowing yourself may bring clarity to you. This commences the journey to self-manage yourself to greater degrees of personal freedom. The concepts will also serve you in helping others defeat their own monsters."

Peter fixated upon the image – the concept that would become a life-giving framework.

"This is interesting," Peter muttered. Jhonny sat in silence until Peter shifted his position. "How does this concept work?"

"The perspective I can offer is this can be a game changer for many MPAs. Here is a quick overview. Your *Personal Sphere* represents you as a person being three-dimensional. You are three layers: the body, soul, and spirit. We desire to be what the Eagle symbolizes: freedom, authority, authenticity, great vision, and the Divine nature. We wrestle with our earthly humanity - where the hypocrite monster lives. Our quest is to soar above like the eagle.

Personal freedom grows when you take radical ownership of each component of your *Personal Sphere*. As you gain knowledge, your understanding deepens. With action, you build the internal strength to manage your body, soul, and spirit – unlocking a true sense of liberty. This is where your authentic self begins to shine."

"Really?" echoed Peter.

Coach nodded. "I see the shift in your countenance, and it looks like the mind is swirling. I am curious how this might impact you?"

He nailed it. Peter's mind was in a blender. "The dots aren't connecting, Jhonny," Peter said. "I can see a path to progress, but the road to growth still has fog."

Knowledge is Key

The virtual beach was calming. Pixelated waves washed over grainy sands, and rigid gulls soared against azure bytes. Peter studied the clear blue water and how white frothy foam burst when it met the shore. Above, a noonday sun shone bright. Either side of him, palm trees swayed in the breeze. Clarity was coming... slowly.

Jhonny asked, "I hear there is some fog. What is coming to you as it relates to your self-management goal?"

Peter described how this *Personal Sphere* model, blended with internal freedom, could impact his world. It was revolutionary to consider oneself 3D – body, soul, and spirit – as a fresh beam of light flashed down... *What if managing oneself could be systematic?*

"Well, I think I can see areas of personal growth that need to happen in each of these layers. I need to spend time seeking truths that affect each component. Now, that may be an enormous wave to ride to the shore, I guess," Peter uncertainly concluded.

"So true," Jhonny interjected. "Perhaps let's start with the basics and see what happens from there. Let me forward you a PDF entitled, *'Knowing and Growing'*. This coaching concept gives you a jumpstart. It allows you space to keep growing in your knowledge of you. From there, we can explore growth steps to take. How does that sound to you?"

"That sounds great," Peter responded.

"I do want you to feel confident in this. Growing in self-management is a continually evolving process. The good news is that your freedom will increase as you jump into action, which we will get to shortly," Jhonny affirmed.

Peter exhaled. He appreciated Jhonny's nonjudgmental coaching style and was grateful for the safe space to explore himself – his ability to offer insightful guidance while maintaining trust in the process. Jhonny indeed had a powerful way of evoking growth.

Peter opened a new window within the software, allowing the document to hover between him and Jhonny. He glanced at the highlighted marks.

KNOWING AND GROWING

Body

- Ownership of your health, nutrition, and exercise increases your freedom
- Self-discipline to engage in an exercise program
  - Increases self-esteem
  - Improves performance
  - Promotes feelings of well-being

Soul

Mind

- A growth mindset overcomes a fixed mindset
- "As a man thinks in his heart, so he is." (Proverbs 23:7)

Emotions

- Emotions are neutral, neither good nor bad
- Grow emotional strength by processing, releasing and reframing life events

Will

- "Guard your heart, for everything you do flows from it." (Proverbs 4:23)
- The power of choice is manifested in Free Will

Spirit

- We are spiritual beings on a human journey
- Spiritual growth of one's Divine relationship liberates the soul

The fog dissipated as Peter read through the virtual PDF. His mind skipped to places where his knowledge needed to increase. Fresh ideas for creating new growth habits flooded in. He reclined back, stretched both arms to the heavens, and declared, "This is good stuff, Jhonny. We are going to need a deep dive."

"Wow. I noticed your whole body just refreshed... it relaxed as you read. Looks like a double shot of freedom was inhaled. There are many layers deep. You will build on knowledge... and grow in truth," Jhonny observed.

"I'm curious what you think. What is becoming clear?" Jhonny asked.

"What comes to mind is I need to work in all three layers. The first is an easy fix as I need to hit the reset button on my fitness. I already have specific actions in mind that I will take."

"There are a couple of other areas to coach through: reclarifying my highest values and being more intentional about living them out. Also, as I read through the *Emotion* space of the soul, I became aware of a need to do some work processing some life events. I feel anger and resentment anytime I think of Craig. Layer in the ongoing relationship crisis..." Peter's voice trailed off as small puddles formed in his eyes.

He took a minute to gather himself before finishing his thought, "Those are heavy weights to bear. A lot of cluttered mind space."

Peter took another deep pause and glanced up at the clear, effervescent blue sky. "And I see increased spiritual growth would help me as well. It seems like I have an expanding list of knowing and growing to better self-manage myself to success, Coach," he chuckled as he nodded his head.

Jhonny continued, "Let's begin with the values. What are your thoughts about reclarifying your values and being more intentional about living them out?"

"I think about Showville. Leading with my three highest values offers awareness. It also evokes personal accountability. Just need to spend time reclarifying them. I will revisit my work in the *Power of U!* course. I will create an intentional action plan which reinforces my values. I will block time off this coming week to do this."

"You sound strong in your conviction. That will fly. As a thought, I have seen other MPAs take one of their values each week and create a specific plan to grow that value within. I have seen them come back more energized when taking this intentional step. If you like that idea, add it to your plan."

"Yes! I am stealing that idea!"

"Good. Let's dig deeper as we explore the soul and spiritual space. If we worked from the inside out, what comes to mind when you think of the spiritual core? Also, you mentioned increasing spiritual growth. What does that look like to you?"

"What comes to mind is a fitness analogy. At FitLife, we coached to help people develop strong core muscles to support alignment and increased body functionality. If the core isn't growing stronger, the body must compensate in other areas," Peter responded.

"Now, going with your analogy, how do you apply this to your goal to better self-manage you to success?" Jhonny asked.

"I just get busy and push spiritual growth to the back burner. I don't consistently devote enough time or space to invest in this. I may reflect for a few minutes to start a day, have moments of deep prayer, but then lose sight of it as the day progresses. I know the days I am committed to allowing God into my life throughout the day; I show up better. I need to prioritize this habit throughout my day. Especially during difficult, challenging days."

"It sounds like the days you deepen your relationship and communication with the Divine are the days you have more peace and strength," Jhonny said, clarifying his thoughts.

"Yes, that would be 100% spot on. Not too surprising, I show up better too. I need to develop better habits to grow in this area," Peter concluded.

"Ok, I know you mentioned the emotion space of your Soul. Can you recall a time you overcame anger, disappointment or resentment?" Jhonny asked.

"That's a tough space. I know I was wronged, betrayed. I am still in the deep brush of it. And it often seems impossible to process it on the spot," Peter declared in a raw, elevated tone.

"I can hear the emotion and the inflection in your voice. Would it offer value to pause and dive deeper into the emotions or explore how you have processed those emotions in the past?" Jhonny asked.

Peter stopped. He thought of the forgiveness bridge he had crossed years ago with his father. He remembered the tearful release of letting go of his self-deemed justified anger. The blissful, refreshing feeling that overcame him. The freedom to not carry the past burden down the road of life. "I would rather stay focused on past success. I think it will offer some needed value. What comes to my mind is my dad."

"Why do you think you were successful?" Jhonny asked.

"Well, I was successful at the time, but I had to reframe the story and release the resentment. Kind of like those truths on the 'Knowing and Growing' list. The truth is I realized my failures and could empathize with my dad's personal story. It allowed forgiveness to be a possibility," Peter murmured.

"Hmm, how could this connection relate to your current situation?" Jhonny asked.

"It looks like I am allowing resentments to pile up," Peter slowly uttered.

"What comes to mind when you say resentments are piling up?"

"The best I can describe it is like each hit feels like another brick loaded up on the pile. And it is getting heavy to bear," Peter expressed himself.

"So my intuition is hearing that each hit is like an unprocessed offense against you that keeps stacking up... and weighing down your soul. How does that connect with you?" Jhonny attempted to summarize it with additional clarity.

"Yes, I couldn't have clarified that any better, Coach."

"Well, is a path forward coming to light?" Jhonny maintained a curious mindset.

"Yeh, back to the basics. Starts with real-time forgiveness. I think I need growth to process these emotions in real-time so they don't stack up. And that path doesn't seem as clear," Peter responded.

"Are you ok if I offer up some thoughts?" Jhonny followed up.

"Of course, Coach!" Peter exclaimed.

"Based on my experience and what I am hearing from you, I will offer up a possibility that may support you. What if you did a nightly reflection? Call it looking in the Midnight Mirror to finish your day. Reflect on moments that brought on strong emotions that left you in a negative space, then work to release those resentments. Finally, self-explore how to reframe the events with a growth mindset. Perhaps daily unloading those bricks you described would offer a clear path. Does this connect with you?"

"That is good, Jhonny. Never thought of being that intentional when it comes to self-managing myself," Peter responded as his countenance lit up.

"Well, we have covered an enormous amount of ground in today's huddle. Here is a closing thought to consider. The greatest barrier to *personal liberty* is the truth about forgiveness. The need to experience it with the Divine relationship, forgiving yourself... and your willingness to forgive others."

"Reaching your max-potential is impossible without a rooted practice in forgiveness. Coach G speaks on this specific truth," Jhonny concluded.

Peter absorbed that truth. He smiled as his thoughts shifted to Jhonny. Jhonny spoke from experience. Jhonny was positioned as the heir apparent of MPA. He spent his upbringing in the ivory tower of leadership with his father, Coach G. He was involved in all decisions... and privileged above all.

As the story goes, Jhonny made a humbling choice to forgo his lofty rights and position. He came down to the playing field, diving into the grunt and grind of MPAs' lives while recruiting others to join the academy. He poured his soul into helping humanity reach its potential. Jhonny's heart to change the world was boundless.

And yet, how often had people rejected MPA? How many had rejected Jhonny? How many committed only to leave at Exitville when the trials and tribulations came? The message of hope and promise was met with rejection. Jhonny's sacrifice deserved attention and recognition. He only imagined how many times Jhonny felt betrayed, cheated, and filled with anger, having been let down by so many people he had poured his heart into.

Jhonny *knew* forgiveness. There was no hypocrite monster in him.

"That is some real sugar... truth," a free-spirited Peter quipped.

"The last step in this coaching huddle is to move from options to Will Dos," Jhonny offered.

"That means what *will you* go do? If you are good with it, I would like you to spend 20 minutes today to write out your commitments from today's huddle. Then send them over to Coach." Jhonny grinned.

"That sounds like a plan, Coach. This coaching session has given me much-needed clarity. Thanks so much, Jhonny. Grateful to you and the team. Give Coach G a shout for me."

"I sure will. And to end on a huge positive, you are almost finished with course #3, *The Power of Personal Liberty*. Just submit your plan and jump into the group training course to complete your learnings. Impressive work, Peter," Jhonny glowed.

As Jhonny stood up and the virtual window began to close, Peter glimpsed an emblem embroidered on his sleeve. It read:

FAITH

HOPE

LOVE

MY GROWTHTIME!

COACH Q

Disciplines. Habits. Routines. It is where the rubber meets the road. They are the difference maker in being able to "show up" and live your best authentic God-version of you.

It can be challenging to hear the voice of growth in the storms of life. Yet, through expanding your knowledge and taking powerful actions to self-manage your 3D being you will grow into the person you inwardly crave to be... with gold-standard character.

That is true freedom. You *will* change the world you influence!

The power of self-exploring in Coaching follows a simple GROW acronym model:

G. (Goal): of the coaching session

> Peter's was to understand how to self-manage to success

R. (Reality): a deep-dive expression of the present reality being experienced

> Peter expressed his struggle to come to terms with people that fell victim to the hypocrite monster and the pain they caused.

O. (Options): navigating options without a fixed mindset to make changes

> Coach G explored with Peter options that would help him grow through his experience. Such as different possibilities to navigate his 3-D being.

W. (Will do): making commitments on what actions you will take

> After exploring options, Peter made commitments to Jhonny of growth steps he would take.

This model will unlock your ability to navigate yourself; a version of self-coaching. The key component is to allow space to explore options without limiting beliefs. From the options, create a specific "growth plan" to build new, game-changing habits.

SELF-ASSESSMENT:

Take a minute to self-evaluate your current knowledge & habits as they relate to your *Personal Sphere*. Use a simple 1–10 scale system. 10 being superstar status:

1. I have consistent, effective discipline in my personal fitness [   ]

2. Rate your knowledge of nutrition and exercise [   ]

3. Your personal mental health and well-being [   ]

4. I navigate life's stress and stay true to my core values [   ]

5. Your personal freedom to live your authentic, best God-version daily [   ]

6. I have a routine to process strong emotions [   ]

7. I practice forgiveness daily [   ]

8. I feel empowered to always do the next right thing [   ]

9. Rate the intimacy of your relationship with God [   ]

10. I have meaningful habits that grow my spiritual core [   ]

GROWTHTIME

Well, those are some hard questions to get honest about. Now, we will develop an intentional "growth plan" to increase your personal freedom. The focus should be on the answers that fell in the 6 or below rating.

- What layer of your *Personal Sphere* do you need to take radical ownership of today?

- What layer do you need to seek out more knowledge?

- Brainstorm specific actions or habits to "know and grow" based on your responses

  Example: I need to improve my mindset

  ✓ Spend one hour to research growth mindset vs. fixed mindset

  ✓ Write out three areas where you are living in a fixed mindset:

    1.

    2.

    3.

  ✓ Commit to journal entries focused on growth mindsets every night for seven days

    Example: I can learn and apply new things quickly. I will learn a new fitness routine and complete it for the next 7 days.

Other growth actions:

- Educate myself on clean vs. unclean foods and their effect on my mood

- Shop on Sundays with a list of healthy foods

- Plan out meals for the next seven days
- Spend 30 minutes writing out doubts about your understanding of God
- Spend 10 minutes in daily prayer for the next seven days
- Write an open, expressive letter to God

  Example: *Dear God...*

ENCOURAGEMENT

You got this! Be intentional seeking out truth. Be relentless in applying it. Freedom is entering your life. Your best authentic, significant-self is about to break out. You will see the growth. Others will take notice. The first step is writing out your growth plan. The next level is sharing your growth plan with another person to increase self-accountability. Create short-term goals in your plan as a path to build game-changing habits.

Oh... turn the page to see Peter's growth plan as you jump back into his *GrowthTime!* journey.

Additional resources are available at mygrowthtime.com

POWER TO THE PEOPLE

Spring Forward

A fresh breeze breathed into his open window as he lay nestled in bed. Softness reflected on Peter's face as his skin absorbed the sun's glare. "The winter storm is officially over!" he proclaimed as he popped up. The fragrant voice of growth rushed in, blowing away the dreaded stagnation. Springtime couldn't have arrived sooner as the seeds of life broke through his churned-up soil.

Peter was revived.

Two scrambled eggs with a dash of salt and pepper, a blended green smoothie, and a slice of whole grain toast – a breakfast of champions. After sharpening two pencils and cracking open his journal, Peter was ready to crank out his personal growth plan.

The first thing that entered his mind was S.M.A.R.T. It was like a nervous system auto-reflex syndrome spent years in rigorous sales management training. All goals must be SMART for success:

Specific

Measurable

Agreeable

Realistic

Timebound

The sister thought about Peter's acronym echoed just as loudly: "Without a plan, you are planning to fail."

So, Peter spent the next two hours with Google and an open mind. After several stops at the pencil sharpener, the plan was crafted:

Core Value Habits

- ✓ Spend 30 minutes on Tuesdays reviewing my list of Core Values
- ✓ Reflect on my Top Three Values and create my Value Badge
- ✓ Reflect on one of these values and create three action steps (repeat for 30 days)

Emotional Plan

- ✓ Journal specific events which trigger feelings of anger or offense (for the next 14 days)
- ✓ Note which mindset–belief is behind the emotions
- ✓ Release anger or unforgiveness by reframing events with empathy

Spiritual Growth

- ✓ Morning Meditation: Prioritize God's relationship through daily study
- ✓ 5-minute pause during lunch and after work to connect with Spirit (for 14 days)
- ✓ Listen to 4 spiritual podcasts to increase knowledge specific to forgiveness
- ✓ Sign up for group training on Personal Liberty today

Peter had worn one pencil and two erasers to a nub. He snapped a picture of his "will dos" and attached them in a direct message to Jhonny. He signed up for the Tuesday evening group training course and closed his laptop. After a confident, deep exhale, he grabbed his light hoodie and stepped out for a long, peaceful walk on the beach.

Peter floated down the gravel path that sunny afternoon. He kicked off his flip-flops as his feet hit the warm white sand. He grinned at the new footprint. Something was transposing. He felt it deep within. New habits were emerging and a fresh perspective on freedom gracefully released from the grizzly winter season.

He reclaimed his top values – Care, Commitment, and Trust – and created his own personal value badge. Each Sunday, he picked one specific value and brainstormed ideas on bringing that value to life. He started with Care. For the upcoming week, he chose to spend more time with his son, Reggie, support his church's homeless outreach on Saturday, and text or call a different friend each day with an encouraging word.

It was an intentional choice to center his values. Jhonny was right; the truth sets you free. The more Peter focused on his values, the less he resorted to giving into a life-sucking judgmental mindset... and further distanced himself from the ugly hypocrite monster. Congruency with his vision was a beautiful beach.

To his delight, he found himself tapping into a well of newfound energy.

The power of journaling became real as he executed his growth plan. He found freedom in processing his deepest disappointments. It was liberating, moving the clutter out of his head and heart and onto the real world of paper. Sharing his burden in the MPA group training offered another layer of comforting perspectives. They added insight to reframe the story... the one replaying in his mind.

His reflections at night in the Midnight Mirror often ended with a heart-splinter cry to God, leaving tear stains on his pillow. Peter tossed and twisted, trying to release the offenses, but the pain was deep, beyond his reach.

It was almost awkward for Peter to invite God into his suffering. He could hardly believe he could cross such a barrier. Yet, Peter didn't retreat... and found true what many other MPAs knew:

Only the Divine could heal a person's broken core.

The 30-day journal experience evolved into a tearful pilgrimage worthy of the journey.

As the days of life unfolded, he was shocked when Divine providence placed a repackaged gift at his home. It arrived at midnight, waking him from a deep sleep. It was a faint sound that somehow penetrated his slumber: *knock knock...* a long pause... *knock knock...*

Peter cracked the door with the latch lock secured. The package was marked:

Handle With Care

A fragile voice came forth. It was Shannell. She stood in humble clothes as the twinkle was restored in her eyes. The sorrow of remorse draped around her slightly built shoulders as she spoke on forgiveness.

The heavens split. She stood before him with a sound mind and gracefully declared how the Divine had mercifully restored her vision. Dark insanity was overtaken by bright light, and the smoldering wick of God's love re-ignited into a flame.

Peter marveled. *But why should he?* he thought. If the Divine could restore the body, could he not restore the soul? It was the second miracle of hope he had witnessed.

The process of restoration was soon budding in unison with the spring flowers.

Peter activated his value of *commitment,* as finding unity was uncharted territory. Work was to be done, rocky terrain was to be climbed, and there was a daily choice to shed the old. They spent many nights praying – intentionally – to build healthy relationship habits. Shannell even rejoined the MPA community she had left behind, her life back on track to his gratefulness. She had lost her way, gone back to Uville, to Exitville, and now she had returned. Peter hoped their vision to change the world together could be restored, too.

The joy of reuniting with family strengthened his soul. He, Shannell, and Reggie were together again – three peas in a pod.

Shannell and Peter decided to renew their vows to build a life, a family, and a legacy. They would soon buy their first condo together just south of La La Land and nestle in for the years to come. Their tribe was about to multiply as two new gifts were delivered. First would come Bo, a ball of relentless energy, always into something and curious about everything; trucks, big wheelers, and cars all made his engine whirl. Sleep was just an afterthought as his party never stopped.

Next up was his beautiful Hazel. Her eyes sparkled like starry skies and her heart was a flourishing garden. She was gentle, compassionate, and full of love. Her passion for pets was unbridled, and her creative artistic skills didn't take long to appear. Peter himself wore fatherhood like a fine set of racing tires.

Ironically, the renewal sprung forth a triumphant letter from Coach G:

Peter,

*Congrats! You have successfully completed the **LIFE** section of Max-Potential Academy training. You have shown up! You are cruising on the path to being a graduate. The next part of your growth journey will focus on the skills needed to be a great 21st-century leader. Your ability to change the world you influence will grow as you embark on this quest.*

Proud of your achievement,

Coach G

Peter's mirror reflected a stronger, empowered man he barely recognized. MPA had changed his life. His roots went deep, his personal foundation was secured, and all things were possible in his hope-filled world.

As Coach G posted about Peter's accomplishment, the news spread through the MPA community. Celebratory comments and likes from his peers dotted his screen, and phone calls blew up his phone.

Affirmation was a beautiful thing.

Rubystar chimed in, too. As a symbiotic extension of Coach G, she even messaged him a coaching question to deepen his understanding: "Congrats, Peter! It has been a joy to be your support over the last several years." Peter paused in admiration at how AI could now represent real feelings as he heard a crack in her voice.

"What can you apply from your learnings to the big picture of your life?"

"Thanks, Rubystar. You have been an amazing support, almost like an oversized comforter during my travails. That is a deep question." Peter trailed off as he squinted his eyes to find perspective.

"Well, I feel like I have more tools in my toolbox," he confidently stated.

"Interesting, how so?"

"From my personal experience, the growth lessons learned in the *Power of Personal Liberty*, coupled with the *Power of U!* and the *Power of Beliefs*... all play a beautiful symphony of music to conquer the dance of life."

"Go on," Rubystar encouraged.

"And these tools will help me help others. Help others live their best, authentic God-version self in this crazy world." Peter enlightened his convictions.

"Sounds strong. Keep running your race, Peter!" Rubystar concluded.

And still... life kept moving. Peter also needed to keep going. He buckled his chinstrap to tackle the career crossroad wedged firmly in his path. And with that, he blasted out of the gate, hunting for his next step.

It was an intense, exhausting three months of filling out job applications, countless resume edits, networking, exploring different career paths, cracking new possibilities, and staying fresh for interviews. Yet... nothing was falling into place. It was a full-time job but with no pay.

Dead-end after dead-end.

Messages from Rubystar trickled in. They were short and sweet, emoji-filled notes about FitLife. Peter dismissed them, but the word on the street was that new ownership was breathing in culture – a culture with new values and fresh vision.

Peter was a skyscraper walled up with caution. Sitting high, all he could see were fearful falls. Could he trust FitLife again? Was it a smokescreen? It was difficult to believe, and besides, how could he go back? That wilderness was far behind, and returning would be a direct assault on his pride and ego... not to mention a perceived regression of his career growth.

The doors of opportunities kept closing. The voice within grew louder. Positive news flashes kept tickling his ears. Past acquaintances and even current team members affirmed it was a safe landing. Rubystar even patched through his fellow and dear MPA mentee Trent, who had endured the waves. Trent confirmed the popcorn trail Peter had started to follow. New leadership had set up a clear vision focused on the Big Three of Business:

1. Team Member Experience

2. The Existing Customer Experience

3. The New Customer Experience

It sounded good to Peter, but still, wasn't there something more for his life?

It was Rubystar's still voice that prodded him. Rubystar was just the support and wisdom Peter needed. She was next-generation technology, an advanced form of artificial intelligence. Even personifying a life form. Peter had given her permission to access his world, allowing her to become familiar with his habits and behaviors. She absorbed information, learned how he thought and reacted, and, in many ways, became bonded to his inner being.

Rubystar yoked her intelligence about Peter to Coach G, providing extraordinary guidance. Due to her ever-evolving AI, her recommendations were based in real-time.

Eerily, her predictive outcomes regarding life events and situational analysis proved prophetically correct. She never violated or compromised Peter's free will of choice or put his car on autopilot. Instead, she offered direction and support in a similar tone to Coach G. Peter valued Rubystar as a perfect virtual assistant to Coach G, even if he didn't always like her messages.

The messages acted like Drano sinking through Peter's clogged thoughts and conflicted feelings. He loved the fitness industry, was skilled in his role, and loved the value it added to changing people's lives. Perhaps reuniting would present a fresh new chapter of growth in his career.

The voice of trust was calling, and Peter knew what he needed to do: take the elevator down from his wall and explore the land ahead.

And, as the career hunt moved at a sloth pace, Peter gave heed to the voice. He contacted Ramero, his former regional Vice President, and invited him to lunch. Two hours later, Peter's fears blew away with the wind. Confronted with his own limiting belief mindset, it was time to exercise his dependent–trust muscle. Perhaps FitLife V2.0 was just the place the Divine had purposed for his next–level growth.

Thank God for Rubystar.

I'm Going to Peepsville!

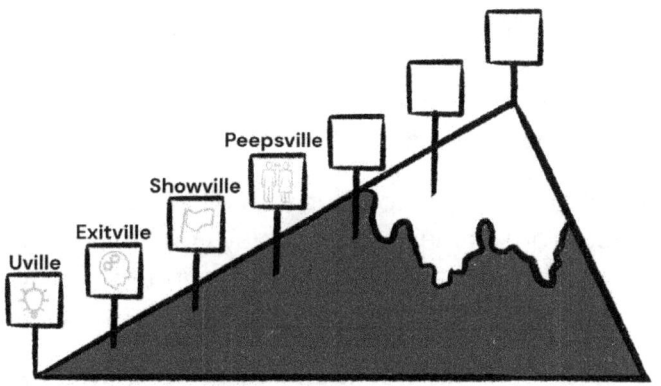

Peter was in a full-court sprint. He crammed a turkey sandwich into Reggie's Buzz Lightyear backpack and bolted for the door. It was a flyby drop-off at Canyon Elementary School before his first day at FitLife.

They opened their arms and pockets as they delivered him the keys to the largest, newest flagship club in the entire market – a true statement of confidence. The fitness center was over 60,000 square feet and decked out with an expansive workout floor, cutting-edge equipment with the latest technology, an assortment of studio room classes, a full NBA-sized basketball court, an outdoor 5-lane lap pool, towel service, and even executive locker rooms.

All the bells and whistles including a corner office with a view to the heart of the gym. Peter opened the door to step over the invisible precipice. He took a deep breath to inhale the familiar aroma. The clanging weights played an intimate sound. The music pumped through his system. The members waiting in line for the spin class door to open drew a deep grin. He was back.

And yet, it felt transposing. The team members at the front desk represented a higher level of professionalism. T-shirts and shorts were replaced with polos and name tags. Peter took notice as he was greeted by Tiesha and Eric, who politely juggled scanning in each member with an effervescent smile and running the busy morning register.

As he gave his new team members a high-five, Peter glanced around the bustling operation. The club wasn't littered with promotional flyers on every wall; no longer masquerading as an unwanted swap-meet.

It was clean. The equipment was all in well-working order, far removed from the laissez-faire days of the past. The new gym was even built with team members in mind, equipped with a break room, fully furnished with a TV, kitchenette, and sofa lounges.

Peter stopped in his tracks as he turned the corner to drop off his bag. He paused to admire the poster mounted on the office entryway. It was a declaration of FitLife's revamped vision and values.

As he admired the vision, a confident voice called out, "Hey, you must be Peter. I am Chuck, your operations manager. We are all super excited to have you lead our team." He spoke with an outstretched hand.

Peter retorted with a smile, "Thanks, Chuck. Glad to be back."

Chuck blurted without pause, "Well, we have heard so much about you. Ramero couldn't stop raving about you. Let me know if I can do anything once you get settled."

Peter's wit responded, "Don't believe everything you hear. Just the good parts."

After a quick laugh together, Peter headed to his office to reflect on his transition plan. The first 30 days were his focus.

His first order of business was a meet-and-greet with each team member to gain their insight. He crafted several questions:

- *What things are going well? What isn't?*

- *What do you believe is truly important?*

- *In what ways can I support you in your role?*

Peter's next step was to gain ground-zero understanding from the members. He proposed similar questions as he met with 30 members the first week.

Peter was impressed with the operations despite a few gaps in team morale and ability to achieve their goals. The club's performance was average – chugging along but not exceeding expectations. Peter had a deep-dive alignment meeting with his boss to clarify some immediate actions and not-to-dos. What stuck out to Peter was the charge to ensure all decisions aligned with the expressed values of the new CEO, Carson Lowe:

Passion, Ownership, Community, and Integrity

During Peter's transitional period, he noticed that things had changed in FitLife. Mr. Lowe was a former naval officer who championed leadership and business development for all his shipmates. His first order of business was to restructure the lines of accountability and organizational flow. Peter was the full General Manager of his team, the Captain, as Mr. Lowe often reminded the field.

The earlier version of FitLife had three managers in one club who answered to three leaders above the field level. The common gripe was that too many captains with competing priorities always left leaky holes in the ship, and the lines of roles and responsibilities needed to be clearer. Peter's managers were responsible for their departments and directly reported to him. Each department manager led teams of up to 20 people.

Peter was giddy with the role. It included the keys of autonomy and responsibility to deliver the company's objectives. He worked over the next several months to learn all the new systems and acclimate to a company playbook that outlined expectations and business processes. He learned how to create personal development plans for his managers. He also went through profit and loss training and read every leadership book Mr. Lowe had recommended.

Peter was intoxicated with growth, a renewed relationship with FitLife, business learning, updated tracking systems, and leadership development. His cup was overflowing.

The team he inherited was diverse: Derrick was his Sales Manager, Rochelle oversaw the Personal Fitness Training team, and Chuck oversaw Daily Operations.

Derrick came from a privileged background. In his early 30s, single, and soaking up the rays. Unfortunately, his charismatic personality was often overshadowed by his rigid, strong-willed demeanor. Extremely talented in sales but engrossed in glamour, he struggled to change and adapt his management approach to his team.

Rochelle was newly-married and career-focused. A former state champ powerlifter, she came from an educated background and had big visions of success. She worked tirelessly, giving without end, to live the fitness brand and find the performance success she craved.

Chuck was a wild card. He was a fresh puppy two years removed from high school, filled with self-doubt about his ability to lead a team. The challenge was that his self-doubt was masked with a severe chip of resentment, a combative prove-it mentality that often reared its ugly head. Peter believed in him, becoming a mentor for the fatherless-figure kid.

Each team member was unique with specific skills and leadership opportunities. Peter prioritized weekly one-on-one meetings and team huddles to boost unity.

90 days flew by. Peter had a pulse on the team and submitted his performance plan for the year. Yet, it didn't take long – a couple of months – for the honeymoon to wear off. Despite his tenacious resolve to execute the plan, his team was not delivering consistent business results.

Derrick's team performance did not meet expectations. Sales regularly underperformed on their monthly goals and targets. His personality clashed with the team; they played lackadaisically in running the sales process. On top of that, his unaware, abrasive tongue often set his fellow managers on fire.

Rochelle's personal training team was on a monthly rollercoaster of results, with highs and lows that left year-to-date numbers behind.

Chuck proved effective in leading operations to Peter's delight. Back-end processes, order points, retail, labor management, scheduling, club cleanliness, and social media support were all on point. Unfortunately, Peter spent his time stomping out flame after flame. The team's customer service skills were crushing his reviews and member satisfaction scores – with Chuck being the main villain.

All this was on Peter's mind as he prepared for his performance review. His stomach fluttered with monarch butterflies the days leading up to the event. After all, careers were made or derailed, paychecks increased or stayed flat, and recognition was won or lost in review time. He knew he was living the brand values, but his hands trembled at the reality of not delivering the expected financial results.

Being a values leader wasn't enough of a warm blanket of security. Results and performance mattered in the business world, *especially* in the high-profile health club he managed. Values were a means to an end, but the end needed to arrive, as a performance culture mindset was still the FitLife benchmark.

He had basked in the limelight of success but knew failure to achieve results left you vulnerable. It was a restless night of sleep the night of the review.

The dialogue with his boss went as he expected. They had a running conversation for months. Peter smiled in gratitude, having received affirmation for the positivity and learning culture he had created with his team. His effort, integrity, and passion all exceeded expectations.

The next layer of the feedback sandwich was tough to swallow as it was clear there were many loose ends: a low engagement score with the sales team, inconsistent results, and a negative customer net promoter score.

The bottom line was things needed to be tightened, and his leadership needed to improve, or... his ship was at risk of sinking.

His boss finished the sandwich with a positive encouragement to make the necessary changes. The review left Peter staring through his office window. Occasionally swiveling his chair to look at the gym workout floor, he tapped the stylus on his Surface Pro:

- What was the missing ingredient to "tighten things" and improve his leadership?

  1. More meetings?
  2. Another round of skills training?
  3. Tougher standards?
  4. Driving the numbers harder?
  5. Perhaps a combination of them all?

Peter needed to fix these leaky holes.

Stuck in a sea of thought, Peter welcomed the distraction of the *ping* of his phone.

It was Coach G:

> *Are you ready for a growth adventure? Pack your bags for a weekend getaway. Rubystar will help you navigate to your destination.*

Peter's stylus dropped to the floor. Just the word *"growth"* allowed freshness to flow into his mind. The voice was calling. And he was answering. He grabbed his bag, darted for the door, and texted his team a quick note before racing home. He was packed in 10 minutes.

After a quick stop at Juice Town, a left turn onto the freeway, and brimming high on MPA confidence, Peter drove into the unknown. His palms sweaty for the adventure ahead.

A hungry fisherman about to set sail into a stocked lake, Peter turned up Rubystar.

Rubystar greeted him. "Peter, welcome to your growth adventure this weekend."

"Yes, mam!" declared Peter. "Where are we going?"

"We are going for a ride out past the Foothill Mountain pass. Just follow my lead and you will arrive at Coach G's destination," Rubystar responded.

"Never been that way. Sounds great, Rubystar. I am super amped about this invitation. Can you give me a little backdrop about what to expect?"

"Well, I don't think I am allowed to spoil the surprise. Just go with a curious mindset and allow yourself space to reflect," Rubystar punted.

"OK, what is the name of the destination, and what am I supposed to do there? Is it a conference?"

"Good try, but you aren't getting anything more out of me."

Peter relented, flipped his cap backwards, lowered his shades, and drove through the Foothill Mountains as the sun hung high at noon. With each switchback through the overpass, his optimism grew. There was purpose behind this pain. His leadership needed an infusion of growth, but what needed to change?

A familiar beep flashed across his dashboard as the sun faded into the horizon. The low fuel gauge was blinking as he had begun his descent. The downward traverse was breathtaking, unveiling a quaint village built beside a vast open lake.

Peter pulled over at the first available exit. The welcome sign was an oversized billboard decorated with a lake view and two smiling fish with captain hats that read:

As he pulled into the local gas station, Rubystar said, "You have arrived at your destination."

Peter grinned at the fortuitous timing. "Thanks, Rubystar! I'm glad you finally spoke up. Now what?"

"Well, I suggest you get yourself acclimated to the village. I am confident things will fall into place," she replied.

"Ok. So, it looks like I will just keep walking by faith."

The village was vibrant, exuding energy and serenity. It was a planned community with well-marked trails and pathways, abundant streetlights, and an easy-to-follow road grid. The picturesque lake was majestic, flushed with fresh water seeping down the mountain range. A cool breeze evaporated any sweat from the hot summer day.

It was apparent that the lake was the centerpiece of life. As such, business enterprises and opportunities were hopping. Restaurants, shopping, and entertainment were all within a short walk. The docks were crammed with private boats and commercial fishing ships. The recreation industry – water skis, parasailing, boating, and jet skis – all blossomed in Peepsville.

Peter learned as an outlet and inspiration to others, Peepsville had its reality TV show on a new local channel called GrowthTV. The channel itself was a visionary pilot where local leaders broadcast 24/7 shows related to personal and professional growth.

Peter was enamored with the concept and noted their upcoming anchor show:

Winning Leadership with Captain Shipley

The show received exceptional reviews and regional acclaim, including three Best Reality Show awards. No dramatization, just real people experiencing real-world situations.

The show's backdrop was following Captain Shipley's leadership aboard his Ship:

Power to the People

The ship served the dual purpose of being an actual fishing boat for profit and an experience for visitors and members to learn about the fishing industry. Captain's leadership took center stage.

Ratings were booming, and locals swore the village would shut down Sunday afternoon to stream it live. The local restaurants and coffee shops had it on; groups met online to chat in real time, and some even hosted parties.

Peter could hardly wait to see if the hype was real.

Savage
Conversations

16

Peter woke up late Saturday morning and decided to recover on the water. He rented a kayak and spent the early afternoon soaking up the sun. Water always had a refreshing way to clear his mind, and basking in Lake Peepsville was no different.

After the lake and a good meal, he was ready to open his journal that night to brain-dump his ideas. He penned out various ways to motivate his team. Contest ideas, incentives, and books he could encourage them to read all seemed to flow with inspiration. Excited with fresh possibilities, his pen arrested when the trailer ad flashed across his phone for tomorrow's Captain Shipley show: "Savage Conversations."

The title jarred a nerve that sent tremors through his muscular physique. Savage was abrasive; savage wasn't positive.

Peter slept on the edge of the bed that night as he contemplated what savage meant. His mind pinged... again and again. Perhaps this was the elusive ingredient. The next day could not come soon enough.

The morning dragged on until the clock struck noon. He grabbed his bag and bolted to the 5-star-rated *Grandma Boo's Delights* downtown to beat the Sunday rush. It was one of many gathering points for the local diehards. He placed his egg-white omelet with bacon order, but his mind was on the big fish he was about to catch.

The episode introduction began with an upbeat tune that sent goosebumps shimmering down his arms: *"Captain Shipley talks Savage Conversations about Own-your-Ship!"*

Captain Shipley had a strong, square jawline, deep brown eyes, and a recessed hairline reserved for seasoned veterans. Buttoned-up and clean-pressed, he walked with purpose as the camera panned him opening his office door. He gave the audience a backdrop as he settled into his cracking leather executive chair.

Peter kept ticking his pen with a fixed gaze at the screen. What did a "savage conversation" entail? One thing he did know was the thought made him unusually uncomfortable.

"Let me get you up to speed," the captain began. "One of my leaders, Davon, who oversees the crew of fishers, is behind on production. I've heard and dealt with too many concerns and grumblings from his crew. They don't respect his leadership and are frustrated by his combative, defensive communication style. The reality is his team is disengaged. I have given feedback with minimal change in his behavior. The bottom line is Davon is great at deflecting blame and doesn't "own-his-ship," as I like to say. It is time for a savage conversation to bring closure to this issue."

Right on cue, a ragged and fatigued Davon knocked on Captain Shipley's door. He motioned for Davon to come into his office. Davon sat down, unsure what to expect from this impromptu meeting. The captain spoke clearly, "Thanks for re-arranging your schedule and making time to meet. To cut to the chase, as you know, your performance results are substandard, and your team keeps resisting your leadership."

Captain Shipley then sat back in his chair and waited for a response.

Davon started tapping his foot, staring at the Captain as he fumbled for an answer. "It's the fisher's crew. They aren't getting the job done," he blurted out. "They don't listen, and as I've said, we need to hire a new crew. Not to mention, the spots we are fishing are terrible locations. No one can catch fish in those areas.

I don't know how you expect me to get results with a bad crew and fishing in bad spots."

Davon paused his rant just long enough for Captain to interject, "Thank you, Davon, but here is the consistent problem that I have addressed. You are taking no ownership of yourself, your team's performance, and your team's resistance to follow your leadership. Your *'excuses with no solutions mindset'* has failed the team. When you do not take ownership, you fail to grow. When you fail to grow, you fail your team. When your team fails, we fail. You have proven your unwillingness to grow. Realize my role is to look after the best interests of this ship. So, with that, I am making a change. Today is your last day on the ship."

Peter was impressed with how Captain Shipley controlled his emotions through the severely awkward conversation – even allowing space for Davon to process.

A scowl of astonishment was locked on Davon's face as a vehement contention of the verdict pierced the muted air. Davon argued that the situation was unjust and that he wasn't getting the support needed to succeed. As his tone escalated, Peter noticed how the captain held his peace, not engaging in his commentary or re-offering explanations.

With no fuel to keep the fire burning, the wake of Davon's frustration began to subside.

It was at that moment that the captain offered, "I do want to thank you for all your efforts during your time on my ship. I hope and believe your best is ahead for you." He graciously extended his hand to Davon and walked him off the boat.

Peter leaned in towards the monitor in awe of the bluntness of what had transpired. What a drop-off point to start this episode, he marveled. That was savage. The locals cringed. Some celebrated as they referenced earlier episodes of despair dealing with Davon's antics.

147

He wrote down three words to describe this savage conversation:

Fair. Direct. Decisive.

The video continued rolling as Captain Shipley called a huddle with his two other managers, Calvin and Esset. He explained the change, "Davon is no longer a part of this ship. Unfortunately, he chose not to grow in ownership, the key principle that makes this ship sail. As you know, performance was suffering. Let this be a teaching moment, as our role as leaders is to make tough decisions to tighten things up. As you know, *'Ship Sinkers'* are not allowed to lead or be on this ship."

Peter's mind reverberated. He wrote down in capital block letters:

TOUGH DECISIONS TO TIGHTEN THINGS UP

What is a Ship Sinker? Peter thought.

The captain read Peter's mind. He continued, "Any leader or player on our team that cannot embrace ownership and display the ability to grow through it... They are *Ship Sinkers*. Let's be clear on this; Ship Sinkers have a negative fixed mindset; they breed contention, suck your energy, deflect responsibility, and refuse to grow through adversity... *They offer excuses, not solutions*. They pull the boat down, sinking themselves and those aboard. Performance suffers, and those fish aren't reeled in! The success of this ship and our mission can't tolerate ship-sinkers."

Calvin and Esset sat straight in their chairs, nodding at the message. Peter jotted down:

NO SHIP SINKERS ALLOWED

This clarified a truth he had been unable to see. He had fallen into the deep waters of empathy – with a high tide of tolerance – without taking decisive action.

He had a ship-sinker aboard, Derrick, his Sales Manager.

Peter's conviction tightened instantly. He had hoped Derrick would change, but his negative mindset and lack of ownership were sinking his ship. The captain's blunt message revealed he was not confronting Derrick with the necessary level of accountability to save his ship.

It was as if he was still trying to save and reform Derrick. At the high cost of his ship's mission. At the higher cost of the team's morale.

Peter's face tightened. A scowl twisted his features as he almost kicked the opposite table chair in self-disgust. His fishing line of tolerance was too slack. He needed to embrace a stronger mindset of "Own-His-Ship." He wrote down a few more notes as he envisioned having a savage conversation with Derrick.

After a long commercial break, which allowed Peter time to devour his brunch, Captain Shipley was back on the air. He took a deep drink of coffee and reclined in his chair. Then he closed his eyes and took a deep breath.

Peter copied him. When he opened his eyes, Captain Shipley looked straight into the camera. "OK, folks. These conversations are never easy, but you can't run from them. This next one pulls at my heartstrings but is overdue. Going to be meeting with Calvin later this week. Calvin runs operations. He is my right-hand man and running mate. I love his hustle; he has the attraction power that people will follow. He gets stuff done and drips with potential. The thing is, we go deeper. We fish together, our families meet up every couple of months, heck, we even play cards at lunch.

"The challenge is Calvin sprouts leaks. His feisty spirit is often at odds with our high standard of customer service. The problem is that he oversees the whole service team, being responsible to make Experience Fishing successful. For your new viewers dropping in, *Experience Fishing* is an immersive excursion we offer visitors to learn what a fishing ship does. Now Calvin struggles to manage the day-to-day grind and be able to resolve the customers' needs."

"Unfortunately, I am the one having to clean up his mess which sucks my energy and the customers'." Captain straightened up. "The real issue is his Pride-Ego. We aren't at war with our customers. I have addressed this before, and he has made small shifts despite being stubborn and strong-willed. Yet, it seems like one step forward, then one step back. Stuck in a mediocre neutral. And that can't be my story as a leader. I can't settle for less than greatness on my ship. The reality is that Calvin has become a *'Ship Drainer'*."

Peter could feel himself being reeled in as he scribbled down that phrase *"Ship Drainer."* Underneath he wrote Chuck, and underlined it.

The screen flashed "Later that week."

Calvin strutted through the door behind Captain Shipley. He gave the captain a fist pump and pulled up a chair before jumping in: "Cap, you see the latest review? We are crushing it. Hey, what is the plan for next Friday night? It's been a while since we have gotten everyone together."

Captain Shipley turned to him. "That was a complimentary review. I'm looking forward to keeping them stacked high. But not to be a buzzkill here, but we need to have a real, honest conversation today."

"Ok, what is going on?" Calvin asked, stiffening.

"I got another review from one of our guests about their experience with you. Give me your insight on how things went down?"

"O-oh," stuttered Calvin. "Was her name Sheila Johnson? She was being rude and unreasonable. She complained about how the boat smelled too fishy, and one of the guests had cut in front of the line she was waiting in. Of course, she was gripping that I was not doing anything about it, typical entitled vacationer. You know how crazy people are."

The captain shook his head in exasperated disapproval. "Calvin, I am going to give you some real savage feedback."

As Calvin sat motionless, a cortisol stress shot raced through his veins. Captain Shipley spoke straight into the teeth of the storm, "You know what stands in your way of greatness in serving our customers?"

"What do you mean, Cap?" Calvin grated.

"You stand in the way. Your Pride-Ego creates tension and resistance in your communication with the customers. That same resistant mindset filters down to your team. That impacts the negative experience customers are having on our ship."

The sound of silence filled the air between Calvin and the captain. The captain continued, "Look, I believe in you, but running this ship is in high demand. It requires excellence in ownership. This is the top ship in the harbor. This assignment may be too big for you to manage. You know we can't have *ship drainers* aboard. That is, unfortunately, what you have become."

Calvin hung his head. "I don't know what to say. Sorry to disappoint you, but nothing could have been done with this one."

"I know, that is what you say quite often." Cap leaned forward. "A couple of options: take a step back from leadership or transfer to a smaller, less demanding ship. Perhaps a step back will allow you time to grow through this issue. Let me know what you want to do."

Calvin paled. Cap's heart felt for Calvin, but savage – real, honest and raw – was the fish that needed to be fried.

As blood flooded back into his ghostly complexion, he quivered, "Are you serious about this? I know I can and will get better; I just need more time."

"Unfortunately, it pains me to hold this line, but time is up," Cap responded.

Calvin gulped but nodded in understanding. Then he rose from his chair and left the office, filled with a conflicted heart. The camera trailed Calvin leaving with shoulders slumped and his chin dropped into his chest.

The video feed messaged:

The Next Day, 7am

Calvin was walking along the long dock as the camera trailed behind. All the viewers in Grandma Boo's Delights were on the edge of their seats. He reached for Cap's brass door handle as the lens panned around and zeroed in on Calvin's re-energized face.

What would he say? Peter wondered.

His entrance caught Cap off-guard as it was an hour before his normal arrival. "Calvin, didn't expect to see you here this early, but come on in."

Salt-drop tears trickled down Calvin's flushed cheeks. "Cap, I did some soul-searching last night. We have known each other a long time," his voice broke. "I am sorry to put you in this position." He sniffled. "I don't want to be the guy who gets cut from the team because of his bad attitude. I will change. I will even ask you for feedback so I can grow up. This is my issue to own. I will not let my pride or ego affect the mission and goals of the ship or stifle my career anymore."

With a lip-splitting smile, a beaming captain responded to the breaking of Calvin's prideful will. "Wow, this is unexpected. You did look different walking in... like something broke. I am glad you are taking ownership. I hear the emotional sincerity that has been missing."

Cap took a long pause. In the savage – real, honest, raw moment – he chose to believe Calvin's breaking would make the transformation he longed to see.

Cap followed his intuition and said, "I didn't see this coming, as your vulnerability has moved my heart. I tell you what. I will support you in staying on." And then, with a quick, authoritative glare, he sent out a fisherman's spear, "But let's be very clear… there is no allowance to go back. Zero."

Calvin breathed a deep sigh of relief and assured the captain things would be different. "I understand the boundary. I just don't want to be called a ship drainer. I hate that. I will even take the online communication course you have been bugging me about. Every week, I will turn in a recap of what I am learning. I will also set a good example with my team. I own my development on this."

The Cap reached out his hand to seal the deal, but Calvin was having none of it. He leaned in for a hug and thanked him for the opportunity to prove his renewed character and commitment to the mission of service excellence.

The restaurant customers cheered in approval. A light mist pooled in Peter's eyes. He gazed in bewilderment. Captain Shipley was willing to sacrifice the relationship with his right-hand shipping mate for the greater good of the ship's mission. That was savage indeed.

Peter wrote down his thoughts as the ads started to run:

- Emulate Captain Shipley
- Bring EMPATHY and AUTHORITY into a SAVAGE conversation

Peter was baffled by the oddity of the segment. It was a mirror of his relationship with Chuck, his Operations Manager. His seat became very uncomfortable. Fear pulsed in his veins. Did Peter have the courage to rock the boat? Risk fracturing the relationship? What standard would he hold to tighten up his ship?

At that moment, Peter flashed back to the whisper trail of the voice of growth:

Peepsville is the Home of the Brave

Own-Your-Ship

★ *Standard of excellence* ★

He shifted forward, grabbed his pen, and wrote:

HAVE COURAGE TO HAVE A SAVAGE CONVERSATION WITH CHUCK

Empower
Your Peeps

17

C oach G had set him up. He could only wonder if Coach was linked with GrowthTV. Perhaps he also had a direct line to the producer, perhaps even Captain Shipley. Either way, Peter felt sure that something greater than himself was guiding his path. Coach G had earned his reputation as being "good."

The crew in Grandma Boo's remained glued to the action with their notepads in hand. The program resumed with a close-up of Captain Shipley's chiseled face walking the deck. A gentle breeze blew his brown hair off his eyebrows, giving way to steel eyes. He directed his strong voice at the camera, "It's been a few weeks since the last savage conversation, but the time has come to confront another one of my leaders."

He took three more deliberate steps before continuing, "I am headed down to check in with Esset. Now, Esset... she is a firecracker, a driven leader." He motioned to a door. "She is in charge of the ship's Client Management System. She leads a team of professionals who custom design plans for the Great Fishing Experience based on the customers' *desires* and *goals* for their trip. She is uber-talented, hardworking, and rather intoxicated with her new promotion to leadership. She has double duty, as she must manage her own clients and lead her team."

Peter sat forward, pen at the ready.

Captain Shipley motioned to the door once more. "I will say Esset is well-liked, and her strong determination resonates with the team," he said. "Yet, despite her aptitude, the team is underperforming.

She loves spending time with her clients, but it leaves her team drifting out to the sea. Here is the deal: Let's level-set the playing field. The main drainer of Esset's team's sub-par performance starts with breaking the principle of *empowerment*. Common in young leaders but needs to be addressed," he chuckled. "If I don't violate my own principle, I intend to avoid being a Mr. Fixed-it."

The captain arrived at Esset's office door. Swinging it open, Captain grinned as Esset typed feverishly on her monitor while simultaneously fielding a phone call from one of her team members. She waved Cap to come in with a pained smile.

"Sorry, Cap," Esset exhaled. "It has been a jammed-back morning already, but here is the depressing update to our game plan."

"Thanks, Esset," said Captain Shipley. "Hey, just take another deep breath. You are doing that eyebrow thing again when you get frustrated."

Peter noted how the captain injected humor into the stress.

"Just relax," said Captain Shipley. "I already know where things stand and the current reality you are walking in."

"Well, you can see the report. I am working my asterisks off and not getting the results I want. Too much effort in and not the right return," Esset said. "I can't figure out why we keep coming up short."

Cap put her at ease, "Let me give you some honest feedback. First, step back and reflect on your team. What are you doing to *empower* them to do their job great?"

"That is a curveball question, Cap," Esset responded. "I haven't thought much about that word as I feel I am being pulled at the seams just trying to juggle my management duties, putting out unwanted fires and taking care of all my clients."

"Yes, your role is complex and has a lot of responsibilities. That is why you get paid the big bucks."

"Well, to answer your question, I give my team daily targets and goals and follow up on their results. I give them space to do their job and expect them to do it. Like they are supposed to do," Esset responded.

"Fair enough. Then why do you think they are struggling?" Cap questioned.

Esset's strong, powerful frame shrunk as her shoulders slumped. "I am stuck, and perhaps I need one of your leadership lessons on empowerment... like you are leading this conversation towards," she said with her own sarcastic tone.

Cap grinned. "Tell me about the clients you service. Do you set expectations for them based on their goals?"

Esset responded, "Well, yes, of course!"

"Do you follow up on their experience?"

"All the time!" smiled Esset.

"Do they have a good experience?"

"Yes, they do!"

"So, what happens between the time you outline expectations and when they go on their experience?"

"Easy. I check in with them often, asking for feedback and offering solutions or options based on their performance," Esset replied.

Cap hummed, "Hope you are connecting the hook to the fishing line. You are the missing link with your team, the connector between the line and the hook. You are playing the role of Mrs. Fix-it right now, cleaning up every mess while still carrying the burden of driving results. You don't serve your clients that way. You can't serve your team that way. You can't do it all and win. You will just continue to find yourself shipwrecked."

Esset's face froze. "You know, Cap. The moment of clarity just hit me. I think what you are saying is I need to save the people on my ship, my team. I must stop trying to control everything and invest my time in the people."

"Yes, Ma'am. Letting go is the hardest part of leadership. Sustainable growth comes not through delegation alone. You can't just expect them to do their job well. Growth comes through empowerment. It is a foundational principle of leadership."

"So, how do I empower my team?" Esset asked.

"The principle of empowerment means giving authority or power to someone to do something and progressively assisting them in gaining control and achieving the goal. Empowerment is about the growth of your team and gaining results through their work," Cap began.

"Do you see how you're violating this principle?"

Esset nodded in agreement, acknowledging, "I am failing at progressively assisting them as I often leave them to fend shark-infested waters without support."

Cap smiled at how the savage conversation was evolving. Esset was gaining clarity as the iceberg emerged. "OK, now that your mindset has shifted, let's put in a simple fundamental coach's play to help you empower your peeps. The Three Step, or 'C3' as I call it:

1. *Communicate* on an agreed goal

2. *Coach* through their progress

3. *Connect* on the result

"There you go. This is your framework. Your growth goal is to improve in each component of the C3 play," Cap said as he handed Esset a small, laminated square from his back pocket.

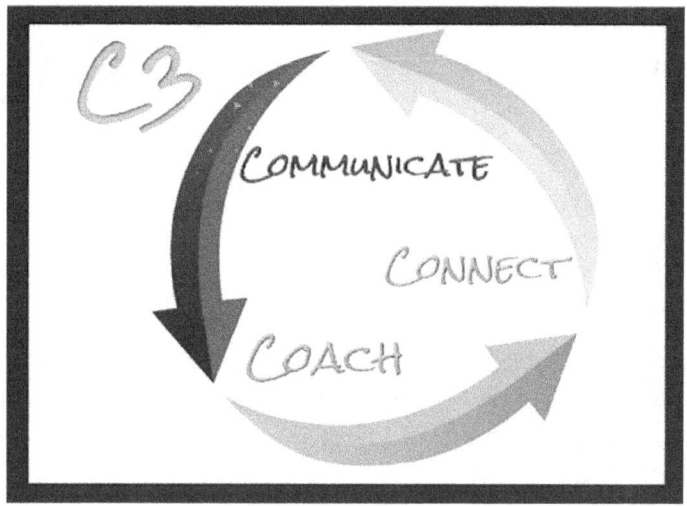

"Now, let's deal with the springy leaks in your ship," the captain continued. "To be clear, delegation of goals is polarizing from agreed-upon goals. Empowering your peeps begins with communicating a goal they agree to take ownership of *and* their plan to achieve it. Include them in the goal-setting process and inspire them to execute *their* plan.

"Next, coach them up. Get involved in their progress. This is the whale of opportunity right in your eyesight. It's your biggest needle mover. Your peeps need your experience. Observe how they are performing, give them coaching tips and consistent feedback, role play and practice difficult situations they are confronted with. Spend time training them in the sales process. *This is the work.* The real growth work that goes into empowering your team."

Before Cap could continue, Esset said, "Ah! The light just went on in my captain's quarters," she laughed, pointing to her head. "I am going to plug the leaks in my damaged ship. I am already ahead on this one, Cap. The first thing I need to do is scale back on my client load and scale up on investing in my team's growth."

"You always were a smart firecracker."

"Thanks for the feedback. Let's get back to work. I have the third component: Connect."

"I love your self-assuredness, but... slow your ship down. I have been watching you – your peeps report their results, and then you react based on their performance. There is more to *connecting* to empower your team."

Shocked, Esset exclaimed, "What do you mean? What am I missing in the *Connect* part?"

"You need to continue the cycle," Cap shot back.

Esset's perplexed countenance caused Cap to continue, "Yes, the cycle. *Connecting* is the growth opportunity to empower your peeps. The connecting part involves asking what worked and what didn't, why their actions worked and why they didn't. As a leader, this gives you clues on resetting, communicating the goal, and developing the best action plan."

"That is great coaching, Cap! That has been a big miss on my part. I will slow down and ask better questions in the follow-up," Esset replied. "Let's connect tomorrow, and I will give you my revised plan. We can review and communicate on an agreed-upon goal," she quipped.

"Sounds like a plan." Captain Shipley beamed as he left Esset's office.

"Well, Peepsville, that is a wrap," he spoke into the lens. "I know this new rudder will steer the ship in the right direction. Savage conversations aren't easy, nor for the faint of heart. The best ship captains embrace an 'Own-your Ship' mentality and the companion principle of 'Em-Power-Your Ship.' Good luck and see you on the lake. Power to the People." He finished with two fists held high over his head.

Peter was convinced he was living in the Twilight Zone. An eyebrow-raising, mind-splitting parallel path to his leadership development needs. He wrote:

Coach Rochelle on empowerment and teach the C3 play

As the chatter among the patrons continued around Peter, he reflected on a reoccurring theme in each of Captain's savage conversations. They were *real*. The reality of the situation was explored and discussed. They were *honest*. Each had a no-holds-barred attitude that honestly assessed the actions' impact on the team or the performance. They were *raw*. There were stripped-down, non-negotiable actions that needed to take place immediately.

The "ah-ha!" moments he had hoped for had arrived in Peepsville. Clarity was a beautiful, gentle flow on a clear, sunny day. Peepsville was indeed the *Home of the Brave*. Peter wrote down his final note before paying his check and heading back over the Foothill Mountain pass:

Brave leaders take radical ownership and empower their teams

Savage conversations are my catalyst to power my peeps

MY GROWTHTIME!

COACH Q

Grab a protein shake, banana, and bag of high-powered veggies. It is time to recharge. This journey to being a great 21st-century leader involves some heavy lifting.

The equation is simple, but the growth work is tough. It is for brave people like you who are passionate about changing the world, the team, and the people you influence.

Principles + Mindset + Coach's Plays = Winning Leadership

It starts with the Principle of Ownership. Volumes have been written; much has been said. The best are bonded and yoked to this word Ownership. The companion principle to power your people is Empowerment.

The major Mindset battle of ownership you and your team confront is *excuses vs. solutions:*

- An **excuse** mindset starts with: "Yeah, but…"

- A **solution** mindset starts with: "This is how I can solve…"

Being "Mr. Fix-it" is the mindset trap found in the principle of Empowerment. You are the answer to every problem. You can do it faster, or you can do it the "right" way, so you do it. This contrasts with a winning "growth mindset." This mindset allows others to solve problems and take action – allowing opportunities to grow and develop. Allowing space for others to fail and learn.

A coach's play is a structured path that allows you as a leader to execute the principle once you embrace a winning mindset. C3 is a great example of how to deliver on the empowerment principle.

Let's get into the growth work!

SELF-AWARENESS

Give yourself an honest rating based on the following statements. Remember, a scale gives you a basic assessment of your current reality.

3 = Almost always 2 = Sometimes 1 = Rarely

1. I confront issues threatening the mission's standard of excellence [   ]

2. I don't allow an "excuse mindset" to exist in my team [   ]

3. I have a good balance of empathy and authority in my coaching [   ]

4. I hold my team accountable in a timely manner [   ]

5. I quickly remove ship-sinkers from the team [   ]

6. I excel at taking decisive action with ship drainers [   ]

7. I am daily involved in training, role-playing, and coaching my team [   ]

8. I feel confident in having savage conversations [   ]

9. I avoid operating in a Mr. Fix-it mindset [   ]

10. I clearly communicate agreed-upon goals and follow up with my team [   ]

The top score is 30. If you scored that high... you are being over-empathetic with yourself! Reflect on your opportunities as you commit to your *GrowthTime!*. Answers marked "1" need your immediate attention. Answers marked "2" require added growth. Answers marked "3" deserve a: "Congrats! Keep up the diligent work!"

GROWTHTIME

Grab your *GrowthTime!* journal, block out time on your calendar, and dig into your growth. Based on your responses, create a "growth plan" to address your biggest area for improvement.

Ownership

- Write out your definition of "ownership"
- Write out an action plan to hold yourself accountable for performance
- Where are you creating *or* allowing excuses rather than winning solutions?
- How will you shift the team's mindset?

Empowerment

- Write out three specific ways you will change to Empower your team:

    1.

    2.

    3.

- Create a S.M.A.R.T plan to provide daily, weekly, and monthly feedback to your peeps
- Where is your greatest opportunity to improve in C3 (communicate, coach, connect)?
- Create a plan to improve

Savage Conversations

- What holds you back from having savage conversations?
- How can you bring empathy and authority into each conversation?
- List the conversations you will have this week to change the direction of your ship

ENCOURAGEMENT

Along this clear path of leadership growth – don't be discouraged. Don't quit. Erase the thought that says, "It is better if I don't have to manage people!"

You were created to be a leader who influences and inspires others to act. Whether by design or default, you are doing that today, regardless of the title attached to your name. Reach for your God-given maximum potential. You will grow in authority as you expand your sphere of influence!

Additional resources are available at mygrowthtime.com

Coach G's Call

Peter shuffled through soft classic pop as he cruised back to reality. He treasured the singers/songwriters of generations past for the stories their hearts sang. They often dealt with pain and conflict, engulfing his own story. The following words crystallized in his mind as the song played: "So bye, bye Miss American Pie, drove my Chevy to the levee – but the levee was dry. And them good ol' boys..."[2]

The ship-sinkers and ship drainers had caused enough leaks in his ship. The levee was indeed dehydrated... dry to the bone. Ownership started with him and all fear must be left behind in a trail of exhaust.

Peter spent the drive back through the Foothill overpass lip-syncing the words he envisioned saying to his team. Rochelle, Derrick, and Chuck had a savage conversation about to sail into their port. His first assignment was to deal with the ship-sinker. Derrick was the first business order Monday morning.

His ship had a new destination called *"Results"*.

Peter walked in sharp at 8am to rummage through his thoughts one last time. He pulled out his scribbled-filled notepad as he tattooed *"bravery"* on his chiseled arm. Derrick followed suit with his typical 5-minute-late stride. A confident breath... and it was go time.

Peter artfully navigated the savage conversation with surgeon-like precision. His voice was calm, firm and filled with a tone of authority mixed with empathetic eyes. Clear statements about the reality of the situation. Candid communication about the honest impact of Derrick's action... and the raw steps of a handshake as he exited him through the door of change.

Deep sigh. Big smile. Peter had done it... the ship-sinker was gone.

Peter could taste the collective exhale of his team, all curious about why it had taken so long. A painful lesson was learned. Next up, he looked to his ship drainer, his go-to person, Chuck. The mere thought of the conversation flashed lightning through his heart. He took the wisdom of his boss and allowed a few days to allow some dust to settle before rocking the boat again.

Peter filled the immediate void. He took charge of the sales team as he scurried to post the open position. His first aim was to restore motivational morale. He infused much-needed direction and a heavy dosage of positivity into the system. He tapped into his past experiences like a seasoned sailor and created a team contest filled with daily positive affirmations, engaged in realistic goal setting, and taught the team new skills.

As his compass charted the challenging waters of change, the day arrived ahead of schedule. Peter shuffled back and forth before reaching for a second spray of deodorant. He closed the door on his notes as gravity sunk in. After all, it was possible that Chuck would be fishing in a different pond after today – adding to the responsibility on Peter's already-burdened shoulders. The outcome was in question. Brave leadership was overdue.

Peter paced his office, waiting for Chuck. *Tick tock. Tick tock.*

When Chuck arrived with a grin and two coffees, Peter skillfully turned to business-mode. After reviewing Chuck's actions on the member service scorecard, Peter was further affirmed that savage needed to happen. Right now.

He executed the conversation like a gem. The message was clear: It was time to leave his post or be reassigned.

Tick tock. Tick Tock. Peter's palms were sweaty, and his heart heavy.

Chuck became an emotional melting snowman in the awkward silence of thirty-six seconds. In the puddle, the virus died. Vulnerability released as Peter mused, "The waxing of the *Pride-Ego released a sweet aroma*."

Ownership had entered the room.

As for his fireplug Fitness Manager, Rochelle, she saluted the message of empowerment. She was fond of Captain Shipley's C3 play Peter shared – Communicate, Coach, Connect – and worked to improve her leadership in each component of the rotating wheel.

Peter leaned back in his chair, letting out a slow, contented sigh of relief. Once again, Coach G had ushered in the voice of growth. Things were tightening up. The production mast was rising, and the team sailed fast to its desired port.

Results.

Team bonuses were in vogue and monthly performance spiffs were handed out. Chuck bought his first car, and Rochelle enrolled in an MBA program. Peter was grateful to stash away some cash for the ever-growing expense of three kids.

People talk, and FitLife was now talking about them. Phone calls from fellow peers began to rain in. Curiosity about how they were winning was on the rise. His team eagerly shared the clear foundational principles, mindsets, and plays driving their results.

Winning leadership was fun again. If only Coach G could see him now.

It was a crisp fall afternoon on his drive home from work when Peter received an unexpected phone call. It was the team MPA hotline. His mind moved into a frenzy. A notification? An upcoming webinar? Perhaps an update on his progress? A nervous energy descended... what if it was Jhonny checking in on his growth journey?

Peter clicked the hands-free button.

"Peter!" hollered a strong, welcoming voice. "It is Coach G, my man! How are you rolling today?"

Monarch butterflies fluttered in the depths of Peter's stomach. Why was Coach G calling him of all the people at MPA?

That was a first.

Coach G's voice was like a jacuzzi jet unleashed, and Peter was the water it moved through. "Hey, Coach. I am doing awesome," he managed to blurt. "Coach, thank you for having me in Max-Potential Academy. What a game changer it has been in my life."

"Well, I am thrilled and honored to have you on the team. I have been getting updates from Rubystar and Jhonny and following your MPA Community thread. You are full-throttle kicking butt through MPA!" Coach G's voice electrified the car's speakers.

Peter's heart pounded hearing the joy in Coach's voice. "Thanks, Coach. It has been a painful, liberating journey, but things are getting sharper as I go... or grow. Adversity has been a good teacher, even if it isn't always wanted. The *path* is *clearer*. The support has been nothing short of supernatural."

"Yes, sir," Coach G exclaimed. "I tell you, Peter, what is clear from my perspective is the fruit of all your growth. Not just the results themselves but also the internal intangibles that people want deep within manifesting in you. I call it the *'GrowthLife'*. You are probably ecstatic that you have a greater ability to love, live with more joy, stronger character, and an authoritative voice that gets results."

"That is interesting, Coach G. I never thought about it in those terms. But I can feel it. Those intangibles are growing within me. That feels cool," Peter nodded his head in revelation.

"You know what I admire about you, Peter?"

Peter twitched, unsure of how Coach G could admire him.

"I admire how committed you are to helping others reach their potential. You are changing the world you influence. You are taking the lessons of Uville, Exitville, Showville and now Peepsville and finding ways to bring them into your life and leadership. Despite adversity, you inspire others to reach their potential... staying humble and sincere. It is the mark of a true MPA team leader."

Peter sponged in the high compliment. His heart reverberated against his sternum. The tingles went through his spine – the depth of authority to receive such an uplifting affirmation of his personhood. Coach G spoke life into his soul. The kind reserved for the power of a father.

Coach G continued, "I am impressed by your response time from the lessons learned in Peepsville. How did you enjoy my friend, Captain Shipley? He sure is a unique character."

"That show was amazing, but how did you know that is what I needed to hear?" Peter asked.

"Well, that is a conversation for another day. But MPA does have some out-of-the-box solutions that we believe will speak to the clarity our members need," Coach G responded with a hint of a smirk.

"The main reason for my call is to give you a huge shout-out for finishing Course #4, *Power to the People*. Your response time in acting on those lessons was legendary. Too many MPAs get stuck at the port in Peepsville – never growing in ownership and empowerment. Just too fearful of tackling savage conversations and making tough decisions. Not you, Peter. You crushed it!"

Peter chimed in, "Yeah, Coach! Thank you for the timely weekend adventure. I must say it felt like I entered a parallel world or multiverse. Not sure how you do it, Coach G, but your methods are effective."

Coach G's grin could be heard breaking through the airwaves.

"I will say parting ways with Derrick shifted the sales team dynamic," said Peter. "What made the message of ownership stick was his team's gratitude for the leadership change. It hurt knowing I should have taken actionable ownership a long time ago. I gave him too long of a leash. A tough leadership lesson to learn, but one I will not repeat. Oh, and with Chuck. Wow! A 180-degree geometric shift in his attitude. Like Calvin aboard the captain's ship, he broke down in tears. Escalations are down, and our member retention is up. Results baby!"

"That is impressive, Peter!" exclaimed Coach G. "How is it going with your other manager?"

"Yes, Rochelle, that little firecracker took all the coaching of empowerment and has built the best fitness team in the market. Best part is she is now in the front of the line to be promoted to a full captain, being a general manager of a FitLife health club."

"It is great to hear your proud enthusiasm for developing your peeps," Coach G added. "Are there any other highlights you would like to share?"

"Yeh, my corporate partners are now praising me for turning this ship around. I even received an award as General Manager of the Year, and my boss gave me a raise," Peter beamed.

"Sounds like you are building a strong culture and growing in authority. That is an enormous highlight to be proud of."

"I am curious, what did you learn about Captain Shipley's leadership style?"

"Good coaching question, Coach G," Peter shot back. "I like the strength of coaching that he exemplified. The strong voice to confront the issues. To live out the principles. And his commitment to his peeps."

"That is a solid observation. A good coach must have that mindset and a willingness to challenge their peeps to excellence. Way to tighten things up."

Tighten things up, Peter thought to himself. How did he know the verbiage his boss used? Odd. *Very odd*, he reflected as he scratched his temple.

"Alright, Peter, celebrate the day as you advance through MPA. You are in rare company and moving at a wonderful pace. Keep changing the world you influence and say hello to Shannell and the kids. I am sure they are proud of your commitment and your desire to be a great 21st-century leader. Keep up the growth, and all things will be possible," Coach G concluded.

"Alright, thanks, Coach, and will do," Peter beamed.

The call ended. Peter glowed – Coach G checked his value box: care, commitment, and trust infused with passion and purpose. He had never felt so connected, confident, and secure in MPA's leadership. He had experienced Coach G as an educator, but now up close and personal. Coach G was an encourager – someone who believed in him, someone who held his best interest, a coach who inspired hope, and a coach who grew confidence in his players.

Gratitude filled Peter's heart as he turned the final curve into his neighborhood.

The Power of
Performance

It's Time to Grind

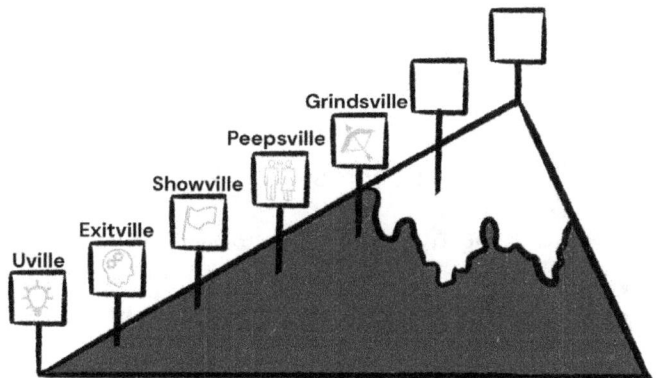

As time passed along, Peter's leadership blossomed and produced a bountiful crop. Rochelle and Chuck skyrocketed. In the blink of an eye, both received rewards for their leadership growth. Rochelle went first. She was promoted to the coveted General Manager of FitLife's first ocean view health club.

Chuck followed suit six months later and was given the keys to a turnaround project in the inland empire just south of the Foothill Mountains.

Peter threw a grand promotion party and vowed to stay connected as a mentor as they navigated new waters – a commitment he honored. The upward movement created a new growth opportunity as Peter went hunting for fresh talent. He took to social media, leveraged his relationship network, and approached current customers to find his next Rochelle and Chuck.

His first big score was Grade-A top-talent Arian Wilson. Once a young, aspiring athlete like himself, he came from a chaotic, fatherless upbringing riddled with broken dreams and toxic relationships. Although his story should have made him a statistic, he never made excuses, embracing the principle of ownership. They meshed well, and the relationship blossomed into a father-figure role, something he seemed to stumble into.

Arian was a cut above the rest. Eager for constant feedback, he speed-lighted from Sales Representative to Sales Manager. Peter had a lion in his den and joyfully fed into his daily skills and leadership growth. Within a year he was promoted to General Manager. Three months later he inked his deal with MPA.

A star primed to shoot across the sky.

Arian was just the tip of the leadership tree. Next came Adam, Leslie, Trent, Sharon, and James. All found refuge under Peter's tree and became next-generation leaders within the expanding FitLife organization.

The flow of talented leaders he developed to support the market didn't go unnoticed. It was Peter's new calling card. His peers often leaned on him for wisdom, insight, and skill development. His boss elevated him to team captain of the market.

As his leadership journey continued to progress steadily, Peter's life evolved. The glue of *commitment* kept him and Shannell together as they shared a relentless passion for their kids and dedicated endless resources to their futures. The expanding role of fatherhood latched onto Peter's soul. As Divine providence would have it, and much to his joy, all three kids fell in love with sports.

The weekends were filled with coaching their soccer, baseball, or basketball teams, taking them on adventures through the nearby wooded trails, wrestling in the community pool or spontaneous splashes at the nearby beach. He took advantage of the calm season of life by planting many seeds of faith into his kids' lives. Daily talks, prayer, and serving the community became life's pillars. His childhood's absent seeds of faith were now infused in his family unit. The lessons learned in leadership became cornerstones of raising his family – ownership, empowerment, and accountable conversations all found firm grounding. Even Coach G's modeling, as an educator and affirming encourager, found new roots in him.

Peter's faith was also on a growth cycle. He had firmly embraced ownership of his relationship with God, coming to full grips with its impact on his life. The work done in the *Power of Personal Liberty* course went deep into his soil, and his core was stabilized. He could see Coach G smiling down.

He took the next step and began to serve and support his local church, investing his time in different life ministries. The kids' center brought out his inner child again, leading discussion groups challenged his knowledge, and spiritual growth courses became disciplines to strengthen his walk with the Divine.

Peter even went next level and started a weekly spiritual growth huddle with his GM peers at FitLife. Just another way he could change the world he influenced using the expanding resources sprouting forth in his life.

Life was good. Steady as a sturdy oak tree, growth unfurled over the next couple of years. A welcomed season far removed from the deserted places and brutal storms of Exitville and Showville.

Seasons do change. Sometimes suddenly, sometimes slowly. The signs of change always whistled through the wind to the ear of the man who stopped to listen. Yet, Mr. Demond was the slow-shift element that breezed in a new season.

Mr. Demond, or as Peter would call him, "Mr. Demon," was a holdover from FitLife's previous leadership regime. He had bounced around different roles in the organization, struggling to redefine his niche and prove his value. Although a legacy man with FitLife, it was still being determined where, or if, he fit in.

Mr. Demond was short and bulky, often displaying a Napoleonic complex reserved for the shallow mind. He walked with a cocky swagger... and dripped with a pungent smell of entitlement.

He was also the newly-appointed Regional Manager, two layers above Peter. Apparently, someone in the Ivory Tower was sold on this reclamation project. It didn't take long before Peter could hear the rumblings.

Whispers worked through the phone lines. The word was spreading like a contagion. Mr. Demond's market tours were a test reserved for survivor island. A mission to uncover madness or unmet expectations, whether spoken or unspoken. He pushed a fine-toothed comb through each fitness center, making countless pitstops to confront, belittle, and embarrass leadership.

The blazing march culminated with his growing tagline to management: "If something doesn't change, then it's time to change leadership."

At first, it was the known underperformers to experience the wrath. The overmatched or disengaged ones. The others took solace in their work, but that wasn't enough. The region was not performing to Mr. Demond's expected results and he wanted a pound of flesh to prove his prowess.

The tours expanded to include all 60 locations over the next several months. The direct messages between partners picked up speed. The noise was getting louder, and the tension was palpable.

Performance anxiety and job insecurity were the new breakfast of champions. Mr. Demond often leap-frogged his direct reports and called his shot: accountability measures, binders, forms, check-ins, and all new standards. Execution was the only measure of success. A hard line, marked by a "pass or fail."

The fallout was inevitable.

Darkness drove out the light. The good leaders felt suffocated or threatened by his intent to clear the threshing floor and left for greener pastures. Others were fired for infractions or oversights unworthy of termination, but many clung on as they questioned the changes.

Peter was left in a quandary. How long would it take for the winds to rise to the top? Surely Mr. Demond couldn't occupy this prime real estate on the corporate ladder for long? Even Peter wasn't immune to the Mr. Demond experience. In a two-hour visit he leveled his team. He tore into James's sales processes, being irate that the team wasn't logging notes to the jot and title as he required. He snapped at his customer service rep Natasha as she juggled greeting members and running the register. Then he miniaturized his service manager for attempting to understand his expectations.

In typical form, he challenged whether Peter was the right man for the job. Peter sat speechless, head tilted in perplexity, on how to respond to Mr. Demond's self-proclaimed style of *seagull leadership* that day – crapping on people and letting others pick up the mess.

The airwaves were now flooded with fear as the word magnified after Mr. Demond visited his gym. Peter was challenged to the core. He found himself muttering obscenities under his breath. This guy, a Regional Ambassador, threatened the goodwill growth culture he had set up. "Who the $%^@#! leads with this type of fear?" Peter vented to himself.

Mr. Demond was right about one thing: it was work cleaning up the mess he left behind. The foundation he had laid took a severe blow as young leaders questioned working under Mr. Demond's anxiety-induced influence. Natasha almost quit, and James's haze of self-doubt lasted for weeks. Just bringing light back into the dark took all of Peter's emotional strength.

And as the year of Mr. Demond droned on, the diabolic shadows canvased the market. Managers were overcome by the blizzard of fear – and conformed to Mr. Demond's style of leadership.

Peter could feel the noir hover in. Many of his peers became chameleons to blend in with *Mr. Demon*, changing colors to match his scowling leadership approach. Their jobs and careers were on the line; perhaps if they stayed low, blend in... they would fall under the radar, hidden from his reproach.

As a team captain, the truth returned to Peter, for even his boss had shifted colors. Fearful of making mistakes, the teams tensed and lost sight of the people they served. Policy and procedures were honored above the needs of the customers.

The aroma of fear and the intoxication of control gripped the region. Morale suffered, and performance lagged. Peter found himself in a wedge. He needed clarity.

A half-day off at the beach was in order.

Peter planted his chair close to the shore. Dug his feet into the sand and tipped his hat low. After a few pages of brain-dumping, he condensed his thoughts in a bullet-point fashion:

- Mr. Demond's pathway is reckless, a symptom of weak leadership

- A fear-induced controlling system strips freedom

- A clear path to lead high-performance teams is undefined

Peter didn't have a clue what the voice of growth was saying other than to *not* lead like Mr. Demond. He reached into his backpack and pulled out his phone. He scrolled the MPA thread but nothing stood out. The idea sprouted to give Rubystar a jingle. Just before he could voice activate a notification splashed across his screen.

Event reminder:

New Offering: Ask Coach G Session

The description popped as he clicked on the event:

An interactive meeting where Coach G fields questions about leadership. Questions must be submitted a week in advance. Coach G will address the most popular ones.

Peter marked "attending" and placed it into his calendar – just three weeks away.

A deep breath. A path forward to answers. Peter started to submit his question when a snap from Rubystar blew into his message box:

Subject: Have you thought about going?

Peter chuckled as he opened the email. It was an invitation flyer for next weekend.

"Here we go," Peter shouted with a fist pump. He knew Coach G was about to sow good seeds into his soil.

Road Trippin'

Peter strapped on his helmet, slid on his riding gloves, and grabbed his shades. After throwing some clothes into his saddlebags, he popped the clutch. The exhaust roared as he piped out of his neighborhood. Fueled with the hope of growth, Peter cruised to the sunny countryside of Grindsville County in his newly-acquired Shadow Spirit.

The hum of the engine purred as he cruised the country roads. His mind stuck on the last bullet point he had drafted at the beach – the need to uncover a clear path for driving high-performance teams. He had heard of the picturesque farm country but had never ventured to the fertile grounds. The early autumn day's warm breeze with a hint of chill proved refreshing. A welcome respite from the grind of life.

The sun lit his path as he rolled towards the first checkpoint of 44Gas Station, located just on the outskirts of Grindsville. Now, Peter was on his "A" game. He had done his Google homework and discovered that Grindsville was a vast open country land, home to three operational farms: Lawville, Freetown, and the Sweetville.

The three farms were the primary source of produce for Gainsville centered in the heart of the county. From all accounts, those who worked and lived in Grindsville County were blue-collar, deep-rooted, work ethic-intense folk – living up to the county motto:

Grind for Greatness

The annual county fair was approaching as harvest time was upon Grindsville. Each year the farms competed for the Best-in-Class awards, which considered three factors: the quantity of the produce, the quality of the produce, and the farmer's team satisfaction score. Sweetville had been on an unparalleled winning streak, save for the great pandemic almost a decade ago that crippled their workforce. Generation after generation took tremendous pride in being Best-in-Class, bringing a competitive fire to the grind.

Peter arrived mid-morning at 44Gas Station and beelined straight for his favorite lemon-lime bubbly water stocked in the coolers. He picked a couple of fresh peaches from the counter basket and scooted into the checkout line. There, he was greeted by a short, weather-aged gentleman with a million-dollar smile tagged with a badge:

Ray thanked him for coming from La La Land to visit Grindsville. As they engaged in chit-chat, Peter was surprised to discover Ray's family was a legacy in the county, having operated 44Gas Station for over 100 years. As the story unfolded, they had partnered with MPA after Jhonny's impromptu visit to the land years ago.

Ray informed Peter that a tour of the three farms had been arranged. Peter was set to meet Mr. Liberty's son Billy in Freetown this afternoon. Tomorrow was a trip to the east to visit Freddy in Lawville and the 3rd day, a tour with Mrs. Candy in Sweetville. Peter thanked Ray for his hospitality before gassing it over the bluff to Freetown.

Marveling at the ginormous statue of the founder Mr. Liberty, Peter entered the Freetown farm. Surrounding his statue were seven other monuments of people, an expanded Mt. Rushmore of sorts, honoring all those who impacted the legacy of Freetown. He parked his bike in the well-marked visitor slot, strolled down a weathered brick path, and walked through the wide front double doors.

Peter's eyes widened in admiration of the elaborately decorated space. The walls were covered in achievement and recognition awards – photo after photo celebrated contest award winners. Banners hung from the vaulted ceiling, marking personal performance milestones from the Freetown workers. Interestingly, a center-piece in the main foyer walkway was akin to a scoreboard, with names and numbers ranking in descending order.

As Peter paused to read the Rockstar Achievement Awards on Freetown's Finest Wall of Recognition, a tall, handsome man approached Peter with an electric grin, "You must be Peter! I am Billy," he boomed while shaking his hand. "Ray said you would be stopping by to check out our operation. Here you are one of those MPAs sent over by the infamous Coach G. I met his son Jhonny years ago. Really good dude."

Peter nodded. "Yes, I guess his reputation precedes him even here in the country," he said. "Nice to meet you, Billy, and thank you for your time to learn about Freetown. Quite the impressive collection of team member awards."

"Yes, indeed. We hire the best high-flying performers in the county and treat them like rock stars – bonuses, contest awards, privilege parking, preferred shifts, exemptions on clean up – you name it, we make sure they feel the love," Billy gleamed with pride.

"Pretty cool. I am sure they appreciate it and others look up to them," Peter replied.

"Well, Peter, not to be short, but I have a jam-packed day. About to kick-off our daily Freetown Finest performance review. You are free to join in," Billy laughed, "or cruise around the farm before we meet up. Any questions I can answer for you, for starters?"

"I am curious about the history... Why do you call this farm Freetown?"

"It was my father's vision. A pun on our last name too. Old man had a sense of humor. He believed in innovation, creativity and celebrating successful winners. He always said to give the workers the freedom to express themselves and deliver performance as they found fit. Look, there are various ways to till, plant, water, prune, and harvest – each leader and team should be free to do it the best they see fit. Treat the winners like rockstars, and others will follow."

"Thanks for the insight," Peter replied. "I am ready to follow you to the review."

As he walked into the packed conference room, Peter flashed back to his early days at FitLife. Two distinct groups, or cliques, partitioned the room. The high-flyers were high-fiving, and the underperformers were already fidgeting in their chairs. The jaws were clenched tight, ready to absorb the next 45-minute huddle of shame.

Billy led the callouts of success as the high-flyers embellished their rock-star status. The bottom performers hung their heads with each missed opportunity of recognition. Billy played to the crowd, furthering the divide by validating success... and admonishing the underperformers' urgent need to catch up.

Peter propped his hand under his chin, stuck in a blank stare. He was all too familiar with the impact Freetown philosophy had on collective morale. Many highflyers stayed to chat it up after Billy wrapped the performance update. A few even spit-shined the boss's shoes. Others scurried out the door.

"Well, what did you think?" Billy strutted over to ask Peter.

Peter shrugged. "It seems like the meeting was focused on the scoreboard and recognition. I wonder... How do you help those underperforming at the bottom of your Freetown Finest rankings?"

"Good question. Our hope is they get motivated, inspired, and put in the grind to be a high-flyer. Unfortunately, not everyone can do it. We give them a couple of months to figure it out. If they can't perform, we must accept they are not a good fit with the Freetown culture... and it's time to hire their replacement. No time for underperformers here in Freetown."

"Ok, thanks for the feedback," Peter offered as they walked the corridor back to the main office.

Peter shook his head following Billy's footsteps. All he could think about were the countless potentially good workers ushered off the Freetown farm without significant investment into their development.

Peter's initial excitement of meeting Billy and touring Freetown withered in this scorching reality; Freetown celebrated the few but didn't grow its population. The tour of the farm confirmed his first impression. The high-flying cliques were uber-engaged, while those categorized as "underperformers" did not gain traction in production.

Peter wasn't surprised to hear the gripes from the workers he met during his tour. They offered their services but were already searching for new work. Several even whispered about applying to the greener pastures of Sweetville.

As for performance, Freetown produced a great quantity as the high-flyers over-delivered. However, their substandard quality affected the demand for their product. Ripe produce took too many bites because it lacked consistency. The team's Farmer Satisfaction Score was tattered with peaks and valleys.

They finished 2nd to Sweetville every year.

Peter had seen similar results from the early years of FitLife's leadership. It was a constant challenge to deliver a consistent experience for the customer; the sales process was not replicable, and operational inconsistencies became tomorrow's headaches. He opened his note app and typed:

- Over-indexing freedom does not grow collective performance
- Individuality does not enhance team member experience
- Without consistent processes, you can't expect consistent results

Peter thanked Billy for his time and motored out of Freetown, looking forward to day two. He punched his ticket early that night as sunrise never failed. The alarm jerked him from a dead sleep. A few groggy taps of the snooze before he freshened up and raced off to Lawville.

There, he met Freddy. The man put Peter on edge. With a cold disposition, his demeanor was congruent to a prison guard's: fierce, stone-faced, and unyielding.

Freddy meant business. Peter's presence was a mere inconvenience to his morning ritual –a farm tour. For the last three years, he had been the general overseer of Lawville Farm. The farm finished last at the Grindsville County Fair, a stick in Freddy's craw.

The farm itself had an eerie, suffocating feel. Brick-thick tension permeated each interaction Freddy had with his team. His scowl accompanied every element of the harvesting process the laborers didn't execute. He was short and abrupt with his leaders... barely making eye contact with the workforce, save to chastise their errors.

Peter bit his lip as he observed Freddy's flow. He clenched his tablet – his walking checklist – as he prowled the fields. Each leader's Key Performance Indicators were highlighted from the prior day. Ranked in columns were:

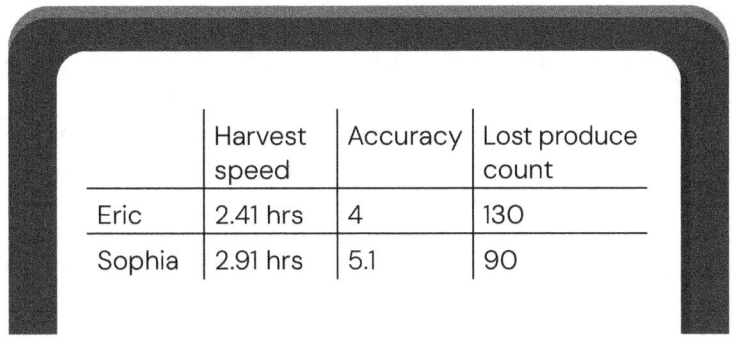

	Harvest speed	Accuracy	Lost produce count
Eric	2.41 hrs	4	130
Sophia	2.91 hrs	5.1	90

Behind in the weekly goals, Freddy frequently stopped to confront his overseers. Snap, stomp the boots, a demanding glare. He demanded increased execution.

Peter recoiled with thoughts of Mr. Demond. Fear was the factor. He took a shot as the prison march tour ended, "Hey Freddy, what is the secret sauce of your leadership?"

Freddy cracked a devilish smile. "It is the process!" he declared. "We are maniacal about adhering to each step. We grind the process and allow zero tolerance for outliers. The process is the building bricks of our leadership."

"Ah," acknowledged Peter.

"Look here," Freddy continued arrogantly. "We finish every year ahead of Freetown in quality because we drive the process. Let me show you the detail we expect from our leaders and workers."

Freddy directed him to the congressional-sized library of reference binders, some paper copies, others digitalized. The sheer volume of Bible-sized manuals, accountability sheets, and Excel trackers used to manage each process was daunting. The cumbersome checkpoints and checkoffs were... exhaustive.

Everything was under the scrutiny of Freddy's suspecting eye.

Peter was gassed trying to track Freddy's infatuation with the process. He couldn't slow the cortisol racing into anxiety. Empathy dug into his veins for the workers, all too familiar with the dark clouds over Lawville.

Empathy was harvested as anger sprouted. Peter bristled with contempt for Freddy's weak leadership. He gathered himself before making a veiled attempt to poke Freddy's bubble, "There is an overwhelming amount of process. I am curious... if the process drives your success, what do you think is causing performance to lag?"

Freddy's countenance shifted. "I need to find leaders who drive more accountability. I have a group of undisciplined leaders and workers adhering to the process. Once we tighten the screws of accountability, our production will increase."

Peter wondered how many years Freddy would be excusing away his high team member turnover and low satisfaction score. He thanked Freddy for his time and broke out of Lawville, shaking the dust off his feet.

The evening restored peace to his Grindsville stay. The birds chirped while a pleasant cool breeze ushered harvest fragrance through his hotel porch. Sipping on his ocean spray spritzer, Peter settled in for the night. He reached for the nightstand and popped open his well-worn Growth Journal. The pen glided across the page:

- *Excessive processes mixed with command-and-control leadership negatively affect performance*

- *An effective process proves consistent results when presented with clear expectations*

- *Elevating complicated processes over the people alienates your peeps and produces poor performance*

Peter hit the light. Morning couldn't come soon enough as he was chomping to visit Sweetville. Freetown and Lawville offered leadership lesson harvests but still had sundried, deserted fields.

Perhaps Sweetville was the answer; the final cog in the wheel to gain clarity. A clarity that would reap the path to performance.

The Performance Wheel

P eter stirred minutes before his 5am alarm sounded off. He sprung into his morning routine, fired up for today's tour of Sweetville. Crushed an on-demand fitness boot camp, prayerful meditation, shower, a splat of crew comb – then skipped out the door. A pitstop at 44Gas to pick up three famous breakfast tacos, gave Ray a shout-out, and he punched the throttle to growth.

The smell of fresh roses and hydrangeas filtered into Peter's helmet as he entered the farm's property as the sun rose over Sweetville. Workers and yellow jersey leaders reaped together on either side of the long, windy entrance. Smiles, laughter, and songs could be heard over the humming of his motor. He cut the engine and glided into the reserved parking.

After wrapping his gloves and helmet around the handlebar, he strolled down a stone path lined with razor-sharp trimmed hedges leading to the main office. Opening the stained-glass door, he was blown away by the team-centric decor adorning the lobby. The walls were lined with photos of the harvesters in action, team events, family festivals celebrating Grindsville's Finest Awards, and community outreach events the team had served together.

Peter breathed easy as a middle-aged bronze-toned man approached him with a warm smile. "Hi, you must be Peter," he greeted him with an inviting handshake. "I am Mr. Nectar. My wife and I are the proud generational owners of the farm. She is the brain, and I am the brawn," he chuckled.

The remaining stress of frightful Freddy's farm faded as his calming disposition eased any tension left in Peter's body.

Mr. Nectar continued, "We have been looking forward to your arrival and have a full day planned for you."

"Thank you for having me, Mr. Nectar. I am just as enthused to learn about your successful organization. I mean, you have an amazing winning streak at the county fair awards," Peter congratulated him.

"Ah, you probably talked to Ray. He is my uncle, so he must promote his nephew," Mr. Nectar laughed. "The truth is those workers and leaders you saw riding in on your motorcycle deserve all the credit and honor. They put in the grind."

Peter liked Mr. Nectar already. He had a confident, humble, and yet authoritative temperament, a strong father figure presence.

"Well, alright," Mr. Nectar continued. "The plan is for you to become Mrs. Candy's shadow. She is one of the finest leaders here on the Sweetville farm. You will follow her, attached at the hip, for the morning grind."

An effervescent, bright-smiled Mrs. Candy turned the corner as if on cue. She took the bull by the horns, introduced herself, and welcomed him to the farm. After a few pleasantries, Mrs. Candy asked Peter, "Are you ready to see how we win the day?"

Peter's competitive grin sprayed across his face. "Yes, I am Mrs. Candy! I love that mindset. Looking forward to seeing your winning leadership firsthand," he exclaimed.

"Well, that is a lot of pressure. I hope I live up to your expectations," she shot back with a confident twinkle.

Mrs. Candy led Peter through the back door headed towards the barn. She set a brisk pace but spoke with clarity. "OK, Peter, the first part of today's agenda is our *'Rise and Grind'* morning huddle. I spend the first few minutes connecting with my team, getting a pulse on their vibe, and laughing about the latest viral Instagram reel."

Peter nodded. "Interesting... May I ask why?"

"Yes. Why the huddle? Well, team building and clear communication. I highlight yesterday's success and advance today's opportunity. Offer insight... and get us out to the grind."

"Great concept and a fun name for your meeting."

As the *Rise and Grind* huddle was about to begin, Mrs. Candy set the tone by declaring the mission of Sweetville:

To Deliver Grindsville's Finest

Mrs. Candy reviewed the day's responsibilities and thanked them for delivering this promise. She revisited the goals for the day, pausing to ask for their input on how they could achieve their targets.

The major goal was to harvest the south section of the apple farm despite the forecast calling for thunderstorms in the late afternoon. Peter noted how team members devised creative ideas to speed up the process by eliminating inactive time between shift transitions, allowing quicker harvest loading. It would be a grind, but they agreed they were up for the challenge.

A moment of clarity came to Peter. Clever to have an informal whiteboarding of options before settling on agreed–upon actions. He opened his note app and jotted down the following:

Give space for team members' input in production meetings

Mrs. Candy highlighted Samantha, who was new to the team, and appointed the veteran Christian as her mentor for today's grind. She then reviewed and coached her team on Sweetville's *"5 Steps to Delivering the Finest"* – their proven process to deliver quality control. Finally, she finished with an enthusiastic rally cry that could have competed with the local high school pep band for top honors.

195

Peter's taste buds were saturated with sweetness as he watched the team race off to the grind. Mrs. Candy's leadership was brimming with flavor.

"Well, Peter, looks like you took good notes," she said, glancing down. "Let's head back to the office for a jiffy. I'll send off a summary and then head out to the field."

"Great. What is in your summary?" asked Peter.

"The plan to win the day, of course! It includes our production goals and targets, our plan of action, and, most importantly, who we are coaching and developing. Today, I am working with Samantha and Christian. Christian is a next-level leader who wants to get involved in management. I will observe and assess how he trains and gives feedback to Samantha."

"I love the concept of including a daily specific growth and development plan for your people," he beamed as he typed another note.

"Yep, that's how we grow here on the farm, no pun intended," Mrs. Candy's voice trailed as she hauled down a corridor. "Harvesting performance always starts with coaching your peeps. It is all about their skill and will."

Peter stumbled as he tried to keep up, not wanting to miss an opportunity to glean this golden nugget. "What do you mean by their 'skill and will?'"

"Oh, that is a mindset Mr. Nectar has deep-rooted in our team. I evaluate skills. Do they have a high standard of skills to do the job? Do they own the will to execute? These tell me about their ability and drive to do the job. I look to coach, educate, and train to develop skills. I motivate or correct if they don't have the will to grind."

"That sure keeps it pretty simple," replied Peter as he forecasted how to incorporate this mindset shift into his leadership at FitLife.

Peter's ever-inquisitive mind was full throttle as they headed out to the field. "So what exactly are you inspecting as you head out to the fields?"

Mrs. Candy glanced over the fence to see the workers hustling through the morning shift. "I start with the good. My first focus is on what is going well and why it is going well. Leading with the negative never puts anyone in a receptive frame of mind. Next, I am looking at how they are executing the agreed-upon plan. Then, determine their self-awareness of any breakdowns or opportunities in the process. Lastly, what is their adjustment plan to solve it?"

"And what are the benefits of that?"

"Simplicity can be more powerful than complexity. These are my coaching points of reference."

Peter gulped the sweet wisdom. Her simple mindset framework was a cold drink on a hot harvest day. Huh, a simple process to coach your team. *Simple was good*, he mused.

"So just to be clear, Peter," Mrs. Candy said, "as I evaluate my people, I can figure out how well they follow the *'5 Steps to Delivering our Finest'* process. Their ability to execute the process and plan will reveal coaching moments. These coaching moments are focused on their improvement and enhancing our productivity. All with the mission to deliver – Sweetville's finest produce."

"How do you deliver your mission?" Peter asked, phone in hand.

"Peter, are you familiar with Sweetville's *Performance Wheel*?" She reached for her phone and scrolled to an image.

His eyes bulged. Was this what he was looking for? A simplified model, a clear path, and a mindset to drive performance.

"No, I am not, but I am very intrigued to hear about it!" exclaimed Peter.

"Great, I will cover it with you at lunch," Mrs. Candy replied.

Peter dialed in as Mrs. Candy went out to execute her coaching mindset. The day unraveled exactly how Mrs. Candy described it. She affirmed the good work, provided effective coaching based on observations, and supported Christian in his quest to develop Samantha.

Pure sweetness.

Mrs. Candy huddled the team together before the lunch bell sounded. She shouted, "Awesome start to the day, Sweetville's finest! The numbers will be in shortly, but I am confident you are ahead of your goals." And then motioning to her Field Leader, she continued, "Deshaun will walk through the scoreboard update after lunch and review any adjustments we need to make. Keep up the grind. We have three more hours before those thunderstorms roll in."

Peter's attention perked at the mention of the scoreboard. How could harvesters have a measurable scoreboard? *Scoreboards are a double-edged sword*, he thought. He had seen them serve as a competitive motivation or a judgment tool.

He wondered about Mrs. Candy's take on the matter as he shared his thoughts.

She readily obliged, "If you can't measure it, you can't track productivity. If you can't track productivity, you can't elevate performance. Scoreboards are invaluable to serve as a competitive, results driven tool to measure success, track progress, and keep us aligned with our goals. Wow, that flowed out just like Mr. Nectar taught me," she laughed. "Cool part... they provide the coaching moments for growth junkies like me."

"I appreciate your insight. Helps clarify my perceptions," Peter followed up as they strolled back to the office.

"Peter, I must say I was impressed with your questions today. It was a joy to have you along for the grind. And as promised, here is Sweetville's *Performance Wheel*." Mrs. Candy handed Peter a laminated page. "It outlines the principles of performance."

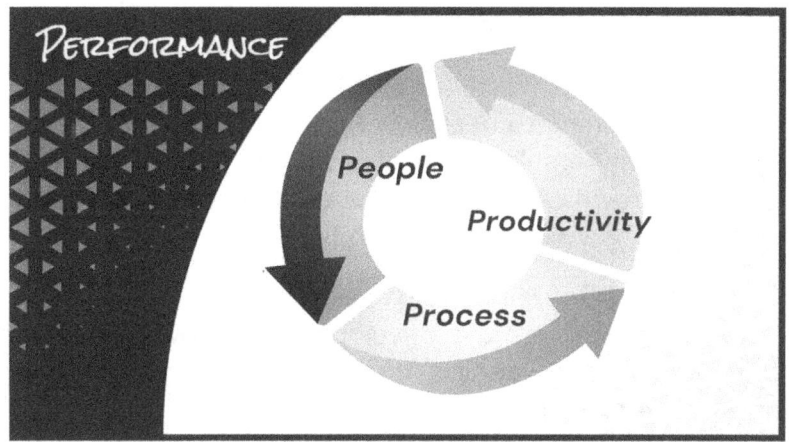

People → focus on skill & will to consistently coach your team

*Process → make it **S.E.T** – **S**imple, **E**xecutable, with a clear **T**arget*

Productivity → engage your team with goals and a scoreboard

Peter looked up to find Mrs. Candy smiling. "The stronger you are within each spoke of the wheel, the faster and further you go, and the results are accelerated," she said. "Just master the fundamentals first."

"Any chance I can take this with me?" Peter asked.

"Of course! Consider it a gift from your time at Sweetville."

"Thanks," Peter said as the clank at the door shifted his attention.

"Peter, welcome back from the grind. What do you think? Did you grow during your time on Sweetville?" Mr. Nectar warmly interjected.

"Well, Mr. Nectar, I can see why your team wins every year," replied Peter. "The quality is delicious, the quantity is abundant, and the Team Farmers' satisfaction is flourishing. What stands out is how the heart of the people is connected to your leadership. The relationship between leaders and workers stands tall like the corn stalk."

Mr. Nectar laughed as Peter continued, "I will admit. I snuck behind Mrs. Candy's back."

"I found it refreshing to hear how appreciative Christian was of Mrs. Candy's leadership. He was fired up on the investment into his personal growth. And he wasn't even bribed for the feedback," Peter finished, glancing at Mrs. Candy.

"That's great to hear, Peter!" rejoiced Mr. Nectar. "That is the area we pride ourselves on most, developing and growing leadership through powerful relationships. I coach on this concept relentlessly. You may have also gotten Mrs. Candy a raise."

"Well, I feasted on the *Performance Wheel* Mrs. Candy shared. It summarizes everything I saw today out in the fields. The focus is on the **people** who run a simple, executable **process** that needs **productivity** to drive results. A good Coach Leader keeps the wheel spinning," exclaimed Peter.

"Now that is a bountiful harvest from the grind. Coach G will be super proud."

"Yeah, Coach G knows how to get the most out of his players," Peter reflected as he rose to say goodbye. "Well, thank you, Mr. Nectar and Mrs. Candy, for hosting me at Sweetville. I am confident your winning streak at the county fair will continue this year."

He shook their hands and thanked them again for their example of winning leadership.

It was indeed scrumptious how Sweetville hit the sweet spot on the *Power of Performance*. With his leadership skills sharpened like the harvester's sickle, the voice of growth had spoken in Grindsville County.

Ask Coach G!

Peter's eyes blazed ahead. His shirt flapped synchronously with the wind as his shades reflected the autumn rays. He kicked his feet onto the extended street pegs and pulsed down the clear highway. His earbuds filled up his soul, "Head out on the highway, lookin' for adventure and whatever comes our way... like a true nature's child, he was born, born to be wild..."[3]

There was purpose through the painful place of Mr. Demond's leadership. The voice of growth illuminated the path to performance. Next-level success was fixed on his horizon.

A Coach Leader... now *that* was an identity Peter could wear like his riding gloves. The *Performance Wheel* was a foundational framework that would guide his leadership direction. The only obstacle standing in his way was how to deal with a Lawville leader like Mr. Demond.

As soon as the brake stand hit the pavement, he scrolled through his notifications, searching for the event.

Reminder: Join us November 3rd at 7 p.m. for the new format "Ask Coach G" huddle:

- *Why: Prepare you for next-level success*
- *How:*
    - → *Submit your questions by November 1st*
    - → *Coach G will address the three most popular questions*

→ *Breakout sessions will follow to include discussion, feedback, and an action plan*

- *What: The goal is to address the questions of Grindsville*

Looking forward to a leadership-changing event,

Rubystar

Peter grabbed his gear, laughing at the fortuitous timing. How comical that Coach G used the *Purpose Plan* concept from Uville – the WHY, HOW, and WHAT – to communicate his message. I guess everything does need a purpose and a plan, Peter mused.

He clicked the confirmation button and sent in his question before walking in to three bundles of love, longing for his attention... and he longed for theirs.

The night of the huddle arrived in a sprint. He clicked on GrowthTeams – the interactive online platform used to connect fellow MPAs via video – as Coach G took the mic.

His majestic voice glowed through the speakers. "I'm thankful to see so many next-level aspiring leaders here tonight. It will be well worth your time. Let's kick it off with one of my favorite icebreakers. Please send your most often used emoji in the chat..."

Peter dropped in the triple bicep flex:

Others ranged all over the emoji universe:

Coach G used the moment to foster a few laughs before switching gears. "Love the participation. Y'all ready to grow?" he challenged the audience.

Peter nodded, blasted 3 thumbs up emojis, and buckled into his seat.

"As for logistics," Coach G continued, "we will follow a new format: a Coach's Perspective and Breakout Sessions. The breakouts are aimed to help you connect to like-minded MPAs and build accountable action plans."

"Thank you for submitting your questions. The focus of tonight is lessons learned from Grindsville as many of you have visited there in the last 60 days. Ray had great things to say about each of you. Thank you for representing MPA well. Here are the top three questions." Coach G shared his screen:

1. *What is the most important lesson to avoid in Freetown?*

2. *I am dealing with a Lawville leader. What do you recommend?*

3. *What drives a good Coach Leader?*

Coach G's authoritative voice rose. "As we explore these questions, let's first level the soil. *Grinding is a prerequisite.* Everyone grinds in Grindsville. Putting in the hustle is the entry point to performance. It's the way you grind that determines your team's success."

"Question one. Let's coach principles as our guiding roots for leadership. At the core of Freetown's leadership, there is a *'freedom with no framework'* principle. This allows for creativity and individuality but neglects the boundaries needed for continual growth.

"They are enamored with the achievements of the few at the expense of implementing a framework to develop the team. A Freetown leader gives excessive liberty for people to do their jobs with minimal structure. There was no consistent, executable process to advance performance.

"So, what needs to be avoided is giving your team too much freedom with no accountable process," Coach G paused.

His perspective matched Peter's notes and clarified this new principle. Other MPAs began posting follow-up questions in the chat.

"I see from the chat that more clarity is needed on the next steps," said Coach G. "No real mystery here; you will have to create a consistent framework in any processes you run to generate a consistent result. Let's be clear," Coach G slowed, "this implies a process for your people's development and product or service.

"If Freetown leadership is your default, and you are over-indexing liberty, then develop your action plan in the breakout portion around creating a simple process coupled with accountable coaching.

Coach G paused and took a sip of water before continuing.

"The second question is a loaded baked potato... dealing with Lawville leaders," Coach G continued. Peter noticed Coach G's countenance shift as he shook his head in obvious displeasure. The awkward, silent pause grew, and the atmosphere thickened with unexpected tension.

With blunt force, Coach G shot, "Lawville leaders poke at this bear. It is a cataclysmic disaster of leadership approach. A leadership transgression. These leaders are infatuated with themselves, full of pride and cemented in ego. Commanders and controllers dominate and enslave you to fear. Fear of mistakes, fear of failure, fear of losing. They present an air of power... but suffocate those under their iron-fisted hand.

"Commanding is not a winning leadership approach. Fear isn't a sustainable mindset. People may hop into action initially, but that same smoldering fire of fear burns them out. These leaders never connect with the heart of their people, and performance suffers," Coach G seethed.

Peter could feel Coach G's zealous fire burning across the Wi-Fi.

"Excuse the rant, but the warning needs to be clear," continued Coach G. "The hard part is navigating this type of leadership, defined by the '*framework with no freedom*' principle. The process and expectations take center stage, becoming burdensome, and don't allow for creativity or individuality. They delight in excessive micro-management as their form of tight-fisted control.

"Unfortunately, there isn't a simple answer as it will depend on the severity of the situation. It will always start with a real attempt to have an honest conversation about your frustrations with your leader. Perhaps the right action is a partnership with a supporting resource or person in your organization. In the extreme, the circumstances may require a courageous decision to leave the team.

"Now, there is one thing you must not do in the face of Lawville leadership. Do not conform to their leadership style. Do not let the fear flow through you to your team. Do not become a leadership chameleon morphing into a Lawville approach. You will damage the soil. Be resolved to improve as an effective Coach Leader as you fight off the toxic weeds that grow in Lawville," Coach G admonished and encouraged his team.

Peter appreciated Coach G's perspective. It strengthened his mindset to manage the elements he was facing. He wrote down the following notes:

- Take courageous steps to resolve differences with your leader
- No chameleons allowed

"Alright, last question before we break into huddles," said Coach G. "What drives a good Coach Leader? The foundation is built on their motivation to build intentional relationships based on growth."

"Let me go a little further. Every good coach wants his team's head and heart to be in the game. A coach must first connect with their passion as a relationship takes center stage. The relationship is focused on their personal growth and development as they drive toward performance goals. It is that Sweetville spot."

Coach G took a breath. He beamed, knowing seeds had landed on good soil.

"Now, speaking of Sweetville," Coach G continued, "I hope you harvested the truth on your expedition. The lesson learned revolves around the *'freedom within a framework'* principle. This is championship–winning leadership. Your peeps need space to contribute their unique ideas and a simple process to follow. The coach provides effective accountability within the framework you establish. I hope that message rang loudest in Grindsville."

"OK, Team MPA, great questions," Coach G said. "I hope the feedback helped solidify or challenge your convictions. Now, *GrowthTime!* breakout groups are next up. Each person will have time to receive input from their peers and develop a next-step action plan. Go put in the grind to be a great leader!"

The GrowthTeams breakout proved to be a valuable investment of Peter's time. He discussed the challenges of working under Mr. Demond's umbrella, his need to improve as a Coach Leader, and the need for consistency with his sales process. His partners asked powerful, qualifying questions to gain understanding and then gave next-step suggestions for proceeding.

Peter valued their insight and crafted his action plan:

> ✓ Get all administrative tasks done by 10 a.m. to free up time for coaching his team
>
> ✓ Daily coaching focus for each team member with a skill vs. will mindset
>
> ✓ Create a simplified sales process using the *freedom within a framework* principle
>
> ✓ Have an honest conversation with Mr. Demond

Coach G pulled the team together as the group timer expired. Each MPA typed in the chat the emoji that best represented how they felt after tonight's session.

Peter snapped:

As he signed off GrowthTeams, Peter's thoughts drifted to his relationship with Coach G – deciding he was a model worth emulating. Coach G had boundaries that were missing in Freetown. He offered freedom from the weights of Lawville.

Coach G had Peter's heart.

MY GROWTHTIME!

COACH Q

Clarity is king. A clearly defined framework is fundamental to your success as a Coach Leader. The principles, mindsets and coach's plays within the *Performance Wheel* are the pathway to winning 21st-century leadership.

Google conducted a ten-year study called Project Oxygen to determine what characteristics people value most in a manager.[4] The No. 1 quality was being a good coach. Daniel Goleman's work in Emotional Intelligence, defining the six leadership styles showed that a Coach Leader is the most suitable for the sustainable and consistent growth of the team... and the business.

Growing into a next-level leader who drives performance *and* meets the needs of your peeps is directly connected to your personal growth as a coach. Navigating the pendulum swing from Lawville to Freetown on your quest to Sweetville will define your coaching performance. The diagram below illustrates the concept.

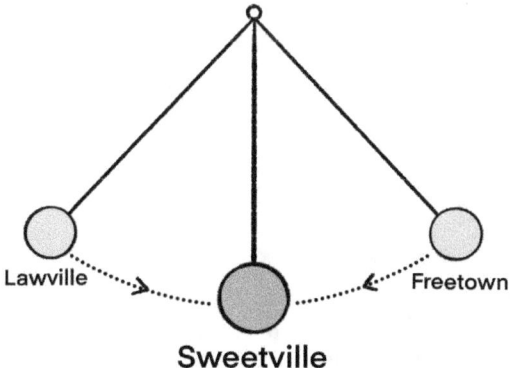

Excessive Process + Command/Control Leadership = Lawville

Little process + Unaccountable Leadership = Freetown

Let's jump into high-value questions to help self-access your leadership game.

SELF-AWARENESS

Open your *GrowthTime!* journal and self-explore the following questions:

1. Where do you find yourself on the leadership pendulum?

2. What steps can you take to improve your relationships with the team you lead?

3. Which part of the *Performance Wheel* needs your immediate attention? Why?

4. From 1–10, how do you rate the current talent level of each of your team members?

5. Describe the developmental process for the peeps you lead. Is it clear?

6. How do you currently use a scoreboard to drive productivity?

GROWTHTIME

Below are three specific areas to grow in your *Performance Wheel:*

People

- List out all the team members you directly manage
- Rate (1 –10 scale) your team members on their **Skill** in their role
- Rate (1–10) their ***Will*** (engagement, determination, desire) to perform

Next, divide your people into groups based on ratings 1–4, 5–7, and 8–10. The lower the number… the greater the urgency to take powerful action, Coach!

Devise an action plan to provide coaching to increase Skill, and clear boundaries to hold your peeps accountable to their Will.

Process

- Write out three processes you are responsible for or need to streamline to maximize performance
- Define or re-define each process by creating a simple, executable one with a clearly defined target
- Ask your team for feedback

After you receive feedback, execute the process for the next 30 days. Check in weekly to determine its effectiveness and learn from the mistakes before making adjustments.

Productivity

- Review the benefits of using a scoreboard with your team
- Discuss behaviors you need to increase production
- Create weekly scoreboards to measure the results of behaviors

Focus your attention on coaching those who are struggling to achieve results and recognizing those who are excelling. A valuable addition is having the high-flyers mentor those who need development.

ENCOURAGEMENT

Congrats! You are making awesome strides in elevating your leadership game to the next level. Don't think you can reap the harvest without putting in the grind. Do the work marked above. Then do it again. Then again. Repetition builds confidence. Repetition is the path to consistent growth results. Welcome to the Grind!

Additional resources are available at mygrowthtime.com

THE POWER OF
20/20 VISION

Next Level

Tere is a season for everything underneath the sun. A time to be born, a time to die, a time to break down, a time to build up, a time for love, a time for hate, a time to sow and a time to reap.

Peter was joyously grateful that it was always *GrowthTime!* Growth filled him up. It felt righteous, meaningful, energizing, and intoxicating. Growth brought wholeness to his life experience. *Hooked on a feeling, high on believing...* his confidence had sprouted high above the seedlings, reaching for the next ray of light to feast on.

Over the next several months, Peter sliced into action with a sharpened sickle. He rallied James, his Sales Leader, and narrowed down the sales process to five steps. James drank from the well of freedom and created a simplified one-page Coaching Guide – less rigid, with more space for personality to shine, and yet a non-negotiable framework. Peter could only laugh when his once confused sales representatives celebrated with a high-five party.

It was Sweetville's *freedom within a framework* of leadership at its finest.

Peter created a new habit, time blocking, to help himself track a daily coaching focus. Clarity had arrived, and he needed to start to think as a leader and not just get wrapped up in the day-to-day doing. His first step was to block 8:30a.m. to 8:45a.m. on his daily calendar to brainstorm the day's plan, which included a team member development strategy.

The *Performance Wheel* concept he gleaned from Mrs. Candy became his focal point. He kept a copy on his desk and shared the mindset perspective with his managers. As the message went forth, focus sharpened. The wheel continued spinning.

The conversation with Mr. Demond went about as well as he could expect. He entered the discussion and voiced his real, honest perspective on the obstacles in the present climate. Mr. Demond shrugged off his comments and doubled down on his Lawville.

Peter wasn't surprised. The walls were too thick to penetrate, yet he walked away with his head held high. At least he had gained a small measure of respect from Mr. Demond for standing tall.

Although the region's forecast was murky, Peter refused to let the ominous clouds overtake his leadership. He remained true to his colors.

The result?

Growth.

Month after month, his team over-performed, team members advanced in their career aspirations, customer service excelled, the people they served got transformational fitness results, his fitness center became the talk of the town, and team member engagement increased year over year.

All signs of winning leadership.

At harvest time the wheat is separated from the chaff. The wheat was winnowed, allowing the chaff to blow away in the wind. The scowling winds finally reached the executive team. In the latest Mr. Demond retread experiment, they made a seismic shift and extinguished his toxic breeze.

The Category Five storm was moving offshore. The evidence demanded a verdict, guilty of lawless leadership and trespassing in goodwill to guide the mothership.

The shift brought a joyous freshness into the atmosphere. Command and control Lawville leadership was officially canceled. Coach leadership was back in vogue. The sunshine brightened collective morale, allowing engagement to blossom. Not too surprisingly, the market's performance went to the next level.

The changing weather patterns shined light on Peter's work. He received a Moment of Magic Award, given to FitLife's finest, for acts of service. The award recognized him as a beacon of light amongst his peers and affirmed his commitment to excellence in supporting the greater market. Patient endurance overcame the elements much to Peter's inner contentment.

It turned out the award had merely foreshadowed the arrival of a fresh season. It was an early spring day when he received the call. The call that completely reshaped the landscape.

It was the voice of Mr. Mustang, the regional overseer of FitLife's Midwest region. Peter's pulse quickened as the words sank in — an offer that would launch him into the next level of his career. The game-changing opportunity to step up as the new Territory Manager in the coveted Heartland market. Peter's knees weakened; his heart knew this was a doorway to a higher place of influence.

A fresh season achieved in the grind.

He nearly tripped as he dashed downstairs to share the glorious news with Shannell. Glistening tears cascaded down her rosy cheeks, flushed with pride for her husband's resolve.

Five years of re-investing in FitLife had produced a fruitful payoff. With two enthusiastic thumbs up, they accepted Mr. Mustang's offer.

The moon rays baptized the day as the celebrations lasted deep into the night. The kids pop-rocked off the walls, and gratitude filled the house for the beautiful harvest the Divine had delivered. Coach G, Jhonny, and his fellow MPAs tagged him with shoutouts. It kept him buzzing to the crack of dawn.

The last message unleashed Peter's inner beast. A sigh of relief was followed by a primordial scream of exhilaration, turning on the neighbors' lights. The celebratory *ping* congratulated him on completing course #5, *The Power of Performance.*

The finish line was in sight. There was a season for everything underneath the sun. Peter never envisioned himself in cowboy territory, but he reckoned it was time for a pair of cowboy boots to practice his *"Yeehaw!"*

With his new opportunity came relocation, which was no small endeavor; even a good change was uncomfortable. Leaving behind relationships and community pulled at his heartstrings, but the optimistic vision of blazing a new trail drove his fire.

The trip to the heartland was a 20-hour sprint to their destination, Hornstown. Shannell, the kids, and their mountain dog had piled into their new SUV – two cool perks they secured with the promotion. Music, laughter... and many bathroom stops filled the ride as they dashed across the country terrain.

Peter's face was engraved with a smile and overflowing with a sense of family pride as they coasted through the oil fields and dodged the tumbleweed. *How far had he come?* So polarizing from the reckless young man who had burned out of his parents' driveway years ago. The song was the same, but the movement grew in authenticity... "You only get one shot to blow; opportunity comes once in a lifetime; you better not let it go."

Fourteen hours in with the kids and dog zonked out, Peter ran on the fuel of anticipation and charged past the hotel stop. By 4am the next day, the wheels pulled the weary crew into their new driveway. The kids' fatigue faded as their eyeballs erupted. It was a ginormous upgrade in living space, double in size with land to roam; front yard basketball hoop, backyard trampoline, upstairs game room included, spacious backyard and a breathtaking sunset view. Reggie, Bo, and Hazel scrambled upstairs to claim their own room.

Peter collapsed on the sofa with Shannell by his side.

Before the first shoots of spring grass could sprout beneath their feet, the kids were already diving headfirst into their new adventure. Their passion for sports continued to blossom, and the club sports programs fast-tracked the transition. Reggie hitched into a baseball monster, Bo had a basketball glued to his hand, and Hazel obsessed over volleyball. Peter's heart swelled with joy as he found himself drawn to the role of their coach, season after season, cherishing every moment of growth.

Peter's new role as Territory Manager marked a significant change. As a profit-and-loss operator, he was responsible for direct oversight of a dozen fitness centers and managed all aspects of the business. His domain included strategy, recruiting, labor management, revenue channels, expenses, marketing, talent development, staffing, customer experience, and team member engagement. He was now responsible for $6 million in annual operating profit, a seismic upgrade in-demand.

Although Peter adapted using what he had learned from previous transitional periods, he came to terms with the distinct differences presented by being a multi-unit manager.

He lamented being removed from the day-to-day production battle and the lost intimacy with his team. He had heard it before: Leadership is a little lonely. Gone were the trenches, the deep connection drawn from hustling step by step in the grind. The trenches were replaced with administrative office days, Monday and Friday, as well as field visits during the week.

A new wash, rinse, and repeat cycle required adjustment time.

Managing independent leaders of leaders needed a next-level ability in core competencies. Growth in clear communication and setting expectations took on a deeper dimension. Many interactions occurred via phone or messenger. He couldn't rely on reading body language but needed to hone his active listening skills. And with over 400 people under his umbrella, every word or action he took was evaluated and analyzed. He was all too familiar with this from the inside looking out. Any misstep or oversight could impact the team's morale or performance. Now, he was officially a coach to the coaches.

The downside was the marginal impact he made on daily performances. As a boots-on-ground single-unit operator, he often inserted himself to affect the outcomes. All the results came through others; less control meant moving into next-level influencing and inspiring action.

Adaptability became a desired competency as his approach to each manager and team culture had to be adjusted. His coaching would need to center on being exploratory to understand rather than exclusively directive. It was a trial-and-error process, but Peter discovered that the next leadership level was about solving problems by asking powerful questions. The questions helped the General Manager and himself discover the root cause of the issues they were trying to solve.

His new boss, Mr. Mustang, was his saving grace. He showed himself as a strong guiding hand as he inserted himself into Peter's world. He took the time to build a relationship. He was personable, confident, and a lover of leadership. Mr. Mustang was the working definition of a coach leader, a Sweetville master.

Within the FitLife organization, he had accumulated a die-hard following and almost elevated to brand status. People gravitated toward him, and his reputation was confirmed. The alignment between the two was heaven-ordained: a similar value system, a passion for developing people, business competitive dispositions, family-centered, and an addictive love for sports.

Peter couldn't wait for Mr. Mustang's quarterly visits to the Hornstown market. Purpose and pleasure were woven together. Peter didn't hesitate to dominate their early morning one-on-one basketball games but was all ears out in the grind.

The second market visit, three months into his transition, proved transformational. The day's agenda was to check in with an underperforming club. Mr. Mustang had Peter take the lead and spent his time observing. Without having to look over his shoulder or fend off a manager's voice override, it gave Peter space to play his leadership game.

Peter followed his plan. He met with Brad the GM first to understand his strategy, gameplan, and execution. Next, he engaged the front-line managers and team members to pulse their experience. From there he went to work offering solutions and providing copious feedback on a bevy of issues.

The team soaked up his coaching...

Or so he thought.

Lunchtime offered a divergent perspective.

Mr. Mustang had a way of getting straight to the heart of the matter. He halted Peter's overconfident inflection of his visit review: "Peter, let me give you candid feedback. The time with your team could be a waste of time."

He paused in true savage conversation fashion, allowing the moment to sink deep. Peter felt his breath vacuumed from his lungs, gasping at de-oxygenated air.

Mr. Mustang continued, "As you know, I spent my time assessing rather than taking charge with purpose intent. What is clear is that you are working on your communication. You are very articulate but talking too much, giving a bucket of advice, and excessive directions."

He took another deliberate pause. "The main message is getting diluted. Your audience isn't clear on the most important actions to take. So, when you leave, nothing will change except people moving in scattered directions."

The feedback shot a dagger at his ego. So much for the affirmation he thought was coming his way. Yet, he knew the uncomfortable road revealed the voice of growth. Peter exhaled, righted himself, and said, "Okay, I think I can see that partially. What are your thoughts about changing it?"

"Simple... work on saying 'more with less.' More with less. That is your new mindset to embrace."

"Well, how do I do that?"

"Well... in this role, the more you talk, the less you evaluate what is happening. The less you observe, the more you will miss the root cause of the pain. Your success is not in being the man with all the answers but in accessing the leadership of the general manager as they do their job. Only then can you provide clear, strong feedback."

"So, on your next visit, just spend the first 30 minutes taking a back seat and allow the General Manager to lead the show. You will be amazed at what you learn. Then say more, with less words."

Peter sat back and gazed up. Truth effortlessly descended.

Any lingering doubt Peter had about the veracity of Mr. Mustang's coaching was squashed the next day. He circled back with Brad, looking for feedback on the main message and takeaways. His rambling ideas and thoughts drove the truth home – there was no clear alignment for expected growth.

"Say more with less" rang loud and clear.

Peter relished the coaching. The pain was worth the gain. This was precisely the kind of feedback he would come to treasure from Mr. Mustang. Coaching shifted his mindset, brought self-awareness, and presented him with a real opportunity to make impactful changes.

Growth was gorgeous.

Over the next couple of years, Peter settled into his expanded role:

1st year: an intense learning curve

2nd year: high-kicking his cowboy boots

3rd year: identified as a high-potential candidate destined for the Executive Suite

Being a high-potential came with coveted growth opportunities. Peter mentored new territory managers. He was entrusted with the keys to leading regional workshops and supporting the executive team with new "pilot" programs. The crowning jewel was asked to teach leadership development programs for emerging General Managers across the FitLife fleet.

The season was pure sugar, a narrow path so sweet it felt like stepping into a world of honeyed dreams.

Cracks to Clarity

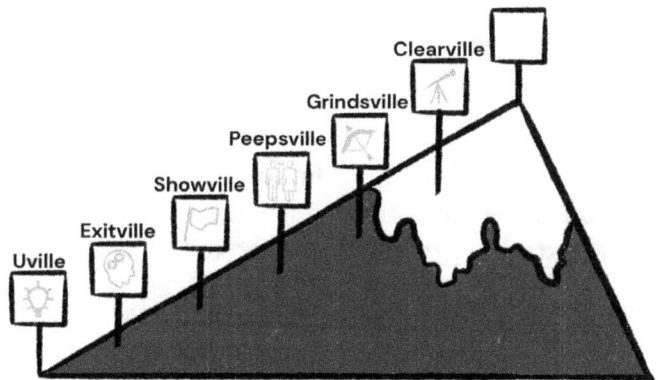

Peter crawled into bed, still suffering from yesterday's leg workout. He peered through the window pane into the stars of the night. His head sunk into the fluffy contours of the feather pillow. He grinned as the guardrails of MPA's lessons safeguarded his ascension on this narrow, clear path.

With the high beams lighting the road of life, Peter beamed, fully persuaded by his ability to handle the curves, detours, and unexpected storms. All things were possible, no matter what appeared on the horizon of an unpredictable future. Fulfilled and focused, Peter entered a sound slumber.

The 5a.m. alarm fire-blasted Peter's stretched-out frame.

First order of the day: House of Gains, Evolution Fitness, and Platinum Training. Those direct competitors popped up with shiny new equipment and fitness programs yanking at his customers' pocketbooks. Second order: small boutique studios began to sprout up with individualized niche offerings that offered higher levels of personalization. Yoga Go, Spirit Spinning, and Booty Bootcamp grabbed the exploding market share that FitLife had dominated for years.

The alarms didn't stop. New concepts kept cropping up. Online fitness solutions and in-home gym products flooded the ever-growing wellness space – capitalism at its finest. The growing competition and shifting fitness trends caused severe cramps for the FitLife team.

The fitness world was evolving, and the consumer was changing. FitLife's steadfast reliance on its brand image wasn't enough. The dust-blazing trail put a financial squeeze on the company that reverberated through its core. The squeeze trickled down as the investment group intervened to make wholesale changes.

The Ivory Tower endured a massive overhaul as the Executive Leadership team was replaced or reassigned. The ripple upgraded into a tsunami wave that washed its way onto Peter's front porch.

It was an abrasive wave to face as his favorite coach leader, Mr. Mustang, was part of the shakeup. The professional relationship, which once budded and blossomed, had been laid to rest. Peter reasoned that some leaders come into your path for a short season, but their impact can last a lifetime. As Mr. Mustang would say, "Sometimes less is more."

Any hope Peter had to be considered for the vacated position was sliced. His new boss was appointed the day after his departure, much to his disappointment. It was a head-scratcher. He fumed, wondering why he wasn't considered or allowed an interview.

In the full-court press of new leadership, his development was shuffled to the back burner. Expanded growth opportunities and increased face time with the Ivory Tower evaporated. Meaningful investment in his future vanished. Impactful feedback to elevate his leadership game was ghost protocol. Career growth was on hold. Peter's fast-forward button was stuck on pause, teetering on rewind.

Peter saw it as his focus being tested. The narrow path was blocked. Stuck behind a slow-moving 18-wheeler, unable to cross the double lines. Fuming at the pebbles kicking up into his windshield.

The scramble was on. Performance results dipped, team members transitioned to shiny new toys, and his entry-level management positions were attacked. Turnover was rising, and his leaders frantically worked to repair the crumbling road.

No sooner did Peter learn a name, they were gone. General Managers were left in a perpetual hunt for replacements. The grind of recruiting, hiring, and training new leaders taxed the troops and performance demands were screaming for his attention. The internal talent pool was moved to life support, and external candidates who backfilled open roles lacked cultural knowledge. The time to evaluate their skills and allow reasonable transition time steam-pressured the leaders, and results suffered.

The path to lead through change blurred his eyes. Another day, another crack – the slivers of glass stuck into his skin.

There was no growth space ahead.

During this forgotten season, Peter heard a rumbling. A still, strong internal voice echoing, *"Cracks to Clarity."* He couldn't explain it nor deny it. The voice was beyond audible, a deep impression that resounded in his soul. Peter called it a *"knowing."*

The *knowing* filled him with comfort, a confident sensation that soothed the blasts in his head. The voice followed him during his drives around the market. He absorbed the message in the quiet of the night. He prayed to understand, but comprehension eluded him. Oddly familiar, yet unsettling, the voice carried the same tone as Coach G's: *"Cracks to Clarity."*

Over the coming months, the downward spiral flattened morale. As the parade of leaders marched through, consistency was crushed. The equations seemed simple:

Low leadership tenure + high turnover = poor performance

Underqualified managers = underqualified frontline team

Peter just couldn't solve this elusive riddle. His heart cracked for his people as they clawed and scratched for solutions: new ways to recruit talent, train team members, and develop leaders. The best practices were shared during market meetings. Yet the puzzle went unsolved as his team fought the good fight and continued to lose the battle.

Change was needed.

The forgotten season gave way to the invisible season as the night realm dimmed his vision. Peter often found answers during his club visits, but they, too, highlighted the spiraling fractures. One thing was clear: each manager took a different approach and got varied results when onboarding new team members. A jaded crack in the market foundation, one that screamed the pendulum had swung too far into Freetown.

A wonderous solace in the noir was the *knowing* was getting louder, "cracks to clarity." Peter just wondered when the *knowing* would deliver on the word. That 18-wheeler blocking his path had to move at some point... right?

Peter internalized the pain. He saw himself as a shepherd, an overseer. Countless members were leaving his flock. Questions resounded in the darkness: *What is missing? What am I not seeing? What can these departures reveal?*

Peter hoped the sleepless cycle filled with espresso shots would run its course. The clock ran for 365 days before a stroke of light began to touch the darkness. His normal Tuesday drive through the crowded downtown 35th street of Hornstown was interrupted by Rubystar's trademark jingle on his dashboard. He answered as he turned down the blaring bass.

"Hi Peter, have you thought about visiting Clearville?" Rubystar asked.

What an odd message, Peter thought.

Rubystar came through once more: "Yes, Peter. Have you thought about going to Clearville?"

The change in her inflection held Peter to his seat. The words sent goosebumps down his arms and shook the steering wheel. Her words felt like the *knowing*. Calmness overtook him. Brightness entered. His hazel eyes sparkled through the rearview mirror.

A transcendent moment had arrived.

As the moment thawed, Peter responded, "I have never heard of Clearville, Rubystar."

"Well, how about searching for it?" she responded.

"Ok, I will. You know... I will do it right now. I just need to pull off this crowded road."

Peter made a sharp right at the next opportune intersection. His mind was racing, and his heart was pounding with wonderful curiosity. He pulled into an open parking lot and fumbled for his phone.

Searching all possible browsers without results, Peter chuckled, "Rubystar, there is no such place. Stop messing with my mind. If it isn't on Google, then it just doesn't exist. Is Clearville real or just a state of mind I need to visit?"

Rubystar answered him, "I can assure you it is a real place. It is known as the underground. It is out in the Hill Country, not too far from Hornstown. I know the way."

Peter's heart bulged, and his veins vibrated. The last words from Rubystar, *I know the way*, cleaved into his being. The knowing had arrived. He was certain of it. Clearville was his destination.

Hope sprouted. Surely, Clearville possessed the answer for *cracks to clarity*.

20/20 Vision

P eter was in a trance when the hustle of life was suddenly interrupted. Time stood still, and the surreal, "*I know the way*" was his billboard. Something had to give. Peter knew he needed a clear vision, as his leadership couldn't allow the cracks to grow any bigger. He clenched his fists, ground his teeth, and seethed.

"How long do you think the trip will last?" Peter questioned Rubystar.

"It is three hours away," she said. "I do hear the night visits get the most popular reviews."

"Well, is it possible to plan to go tonight? Fortuitous timing, with the family out of town visiting friends. Other than catching up on sleep, I am wide open. I can finish up work, grab a bite, and then head for the hills."

"Not an issue. I will message ahead to gain access to the city," she responded.

"Access to the city?" Peter hummed. "What kind of place are you taking me to?"

"Have I ever let you down?"

"No, but I am not sure what this is leading to... but you have never failed me yet."

"We sure haven't," Rubystar affirmed.

Peter closed out the day with a weekly recap email to his team. He tore through a hot chicken drive-thru, punching the gas as he launched into the uncharted hill country. The journey was laced with a sweet aroma, each mile dripping with the promise of what lay ahead.

The sky dimmed to evening, and a beautiful sense of anticipation permeated the air. Each mile elevated a heightened foretaste of encountering the extraordinary. Peter carved the country road through one tree-covered hill after another, journeying up, down, and around the ascending terrain.

Fully at ease, trusting in the voice of Rubystar and guided by the moonbeams slipping through the cloudy sky. A glowing light in the distance captured his eyes. He knew it was Clearville.

With a diaphragm-relaxing exhale, Peter cornered the final turn to exit the darkness. His eyes glimmered at the perfectly straight, breathtaking road that ascended to a beacon of light. The steep incline was lined with effervescent post lamps, each engraved with the letter "C" leading up to a massive city gate. Captivated by the crisp star-like shine of the road leading to the revealed monstrosity of Clearville, Peter's wheels glided as he approached the gate.

The city on the hill was anchored to the earth, content to emit its shine into the coolness of the night. Distinguished, illuminated, grandiose... Peter felt small yet oddly still significant.

As Peter approached the steel-enforced walls, he smiled at the sign:

Welcome to Clearville

The next flash declared:

A third flash radiated in bold white letters:

Peter's jaw fell open as he arrived at the gate. He reached for the window controls, ready to speak to the impeccably dressed attendant, as the ping resonated through the still air.

> *Peter! Heard you have arrived in Clearville. I called in a favor, and you will have full access to explore the city. Observe all the sights, sounds, and actions. Quite an extraordinary place. Hope things clear up in Clearville* 😊
>
> *— Jhonny*

Peter laughed as the attendant tipped his hat. The city's streets were glistening as with white sapphire. The buildings boasted marble, granite, slate, gold, cedar, sandalwood, and glass. Each was a work of art, designed and decorated with expert craftsmanship.

Botanical gardens and foliage lined the spacious roads. The well-groomed homes were just outside a classic downtown section of the city. The foundation itself was laid upon granite, strong and pristine. Clearville was built as a testimony to all.

What stood out to Peter was an enormous clock constructed in the middle of Clearville. When the clock struck the hour, the Clearville mission was heralded throughout the city:

We bring clarity to all by pursuing excellence together.

It was a wonderful, majestic sound pulsating through Peter's soul. He noticed the groundskeepers paying uncommon attention to detail as they vacuumed the streets. No chewing wrapper was left behind, trash can tipped over, or mess left unswept. The crew moved with seamless precision, their actions flowing effortlessly as they carried out their tasks. Their communication was fluent, with an intuitive rhythm that guided the work. Their polo sleeves were garnished with a tightly embroidered mission logo:

Bringing Clarity to All

Peter even glimpsed their sparkling bracelets stamped with:

Pursuing Excellence Together

How interesting, Peter thought. He continued on, wrapping through the central roundabout. There a group of people wandering just outside the city wall caught his attention, longing to enter. They shouldered large backpacks, wearing exhaustion. Peter noticed their faces – red eyes and empty stares. Their groans and utterings were beyond comprehension. His face shifted to a frown as several members turned away and began descending a darkening path on the hill, giving up on the city.

Now parked at the west gate, stillness invaded Peter as room for understanding entered. He could hear the *knowing* whisper in the stillness, "Without a vision, the people perish."

Dumbstruck, the parallel worlds violently collided, and a revelation broke forth. *My team is missing a fresh, clear vision...* Peter thought of the countless hires who had left. The painful truth manifested: *My leadership was the gatekeeper to the city. I was the roadblock in leading through change.*

The cracks were moving to clarity.

Peter wrote down a few notes on vision. He shifted gears to drive and exited through the west gate thinking of his next steps as he headed back to Hornstown.

Peter cruised along the outskirts back to the east gate. He thought the voice of growth had finished speaking, but it hadn't. His pulse spiked as he caught sight of a man standing in defiant protest. The young, battered man created a raucous commotion near the north gate. Armed with bricks and bottles, he was prepared to start a one-man war. He lobbied for justice and his right to live in the city.

There was a sign draped over his head that read:

I belong

A small brigade of Clearville's finest masked with protective gear stood their ground, uncertain of the man's next step. Peter watched from afar as a confrontational showdown seemed imminent to erupt.

Suddenly, Peter saw a beam of light from the watchtower bless the man's enraged face. The man froze like a deer in headlights. The ray buckled the man to the ground, reducing him to a heap.

The man abruptly arose. A sense of sanity overshadowed him, and a calm peace descended on his face. He removed his sign, pushed his bricks aside, and floated toward a narrow bridge. It was an unobstructed passage over the wall into Clearville. Once he arrived, he touched down and skipped across.

It was a showstopper for Peter as the *knowing* descended like the morning dew. A washing away of his blindness. He was that *man*.

The metaphor was clear. He was consumed with his career growth being derailed – a block to the Ivory Tower of leadership. The unresolved internal strain was causing him to lose focus on his true mission. His mission wasn't about climbing high in FitLife but impacting one person at a time to reach their potential.

Simply changing the world he influenced.

A tainted vision. Cracks from within. Blurring the bridge to clarity. He bounced his head on the steering wheel. This 18-wheeler wasn't meant to go around but to soar above. Only the wings of an eagle could give him a new perspective.

Peter unbuckled his seat belt, reclined back, and peered through the sunroof. The moonbeams shone against his cheeks. His spirit was renewed, and a new determination overcame him. He had to go deeper, not wider, into his market to develop leaders, investing his resources down to those standing outside the gate – the ones desperate to enter. He vowed that his quest to develop leaders' lives would extend past his immediate direct reports and flow deeper to those who needed access to a Clearville: *a clear vision, a unified language, and a solid foundation.*

All the majestic leadership qualities Clearville offered in pursuit of excellence.

The cracks were moving to clear 20/20 vision.

The Next Day

The canopy of clouds peeled back, revealing the starry hosts of heaven as Peter waved goodbye to the gate attendant. The road glowed as he glanced at the majestic center that sparkled in his rearview mirror. He cracked his window, letting in the gentle chirp of insects that created a soothing backdrop to the serene stillness of the night.

Inside the spacious container of Peter's mind, the thoughts ricocheted like Powerball Lottery *pings*, each sparking ideas across his neurons. One *ping* challenged his mindset on leadership. Another *ping* illuminated possible pitfalls. A third *ping* opened pathways he had never considered.

Rubystar's crystal-clear voice interrupted the pings, "Peter, would you like a sounding board to help with the process?"

"Hey Rubystar, you are in my head!" proclaimed Peter. "My mind is *pinging*... and there has to be a winning ticket."

"OK, I can pull high-value questions from my resources to help organize those pings. I can reorganize your responses and then email them to you. How does that sound?"

"Sounds like AI Rubystar at its finest," Peter cracked. "We've got a long trip through the early morning hours, so let's chat through it."

"Great, what stood out to you from the beginning?"

"The passage through the gate. Specifically, Jhonny's message to *'observe the sights, sounds, actions'* were obvious parallels.

The foundation with my team at FitLife is not built on a solid foundation like Clearville. I am spending too much energy plugging holes and filling gaps rather than having a solid visionary platform for the market. There is no base to build on, and all the results fall through the cracks."

"How can you start to build a vision?"

"That is the question that is playing bouncy ball upstairs. I do know that times are changing and I need to lead better through change. The next generation of peeps we are hiring are looking for more. They long for Clearville, connecting to a meaningful vision, not just the grind. What comes to mind is partnering with my managers and crafting a fresh vision statement. Something that will bring in the money," Peter laughed.

"What would bring in the money?"

"What comes to mind is an old catchphrase I recall... a *'Phrase that Pays.'* It would be a visionary mantra like Clearville's *Bringing Clarity to All'*."

"That sounds clever – catchy. What else is pinging around?"

"The night crew and those people drifting at the east gate showed another chip in the foundation. The night crew had a seamless flow with their communication to get stuff done. On the flip side, I couldn't understand the dialect of the gate people; they spoke in an unknown tongue and didn't go anywhere. What comes to mind is that I must form a common language with which all can identify. Perhaps narrow down the language into three key focus items."

"That's good," Rubystar said. "Where do your thoughts go from there?"

"Get those words embedded into their mindset, creating a unified focus," Peter answered. "Oh, and the clock tower... Yeah! A vision is good if people hear about it. I need to herald the new vision. Start speaking inspiration into the day-to-day grind."

"Sounds like you are building a new foundation," Rubystar furthered the thought. "How can you bring that concept to your team?"

"I am not fully clear on that." Peter shook his head.

"Take a pause, close your eyes, and visualize it. Look for a picture or image representing what you are seeing."

"Ok, let me pull over. Pretty sure closing your eyes and driving is some type of violation," Peter added in lighthearted humor.

"You are definitely thinking clearly now," Rubystar quipped.

Just ahead was a rest stop that overlooked the hill country. He pulled into the gravel-lined safety zone, swung open the door, and unfolded his legs as he made his way toward the guardrail overlooking the vista. Exploring himself through visualization felt unfamiliar and uncomfortable, but he was willing to give it a shot – especially when the idea came from someone he trusted deeply, like Rubystar.

The transcendent scenic view and the refreshing breeze brought peace within. Peter relaxed his shoulders, opened his palms to the heavens, and inhaled the depth of clarity before exhaling a silent prayer.

Inhale... Exhale... Inhale...

Light flooded in, and the pings abruptly ceased. An image etched itself against the darkness of his closed eyelids. In that instant, he knew. Peter opened his eyes as a star flashed across the sky. He broke into a short sprint, kicking up gravel as he raced back to the car. With an unbridled shout, he exclaimed, "I've got it, Rubystar!"

"What popped into your mind, Peter?" Rubystar responded in anticipation.

"I saw the image of an Olympic champion standing on an elevated two-layer platform. The champion was standing on the platform, holding up the eternal fire of the Olympic torch. The image was in the form of a pyramid."

"That is inspiring. What symbolism do you draw from it?"

"I'm not sure. Let me stretch it out," Peter replied as he reached for his backpack. His heart was on fire as the winning ticket divinely fell into his pocket.

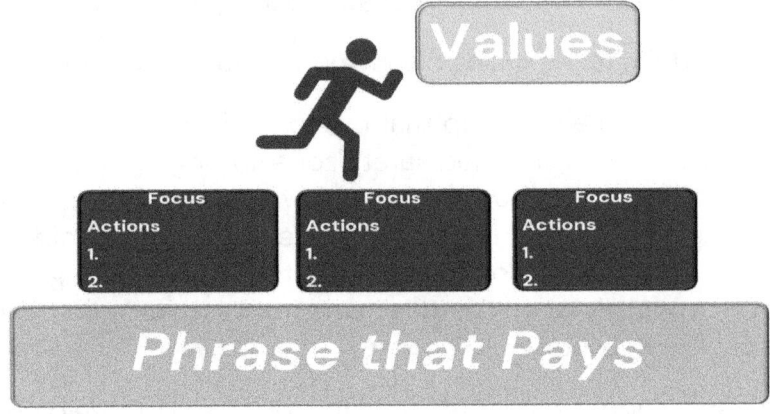

"This is how I see the vision, Rubystar. First, we build a new foundation rooted in our core motivator – the *'Phrase that Pays,'* our WHY as a team. The next step is to create a unified language around the key focus areas that will drive our success. Our team champions can lead this charge, fueled by the fire of our shared values – values I learned in Showville and have seen fully realized in Clearville.

"That sounds like visionary leadership to me," proclaimed Rubystar.

Peter paused as the numbers in his Powerball aligned, "This is the winning ticket, Rubystar!"

"The revelatory ideas are flowing, and my mindset is crystallizing. Hard to believe I couldn't see this before. Take this note, Rubystar." Peter sat tall. "My team must be connected to a mission that transcends themselves. A vision that moves past their motives and limitations and bonds them to the greater calling. We will lead with vision and then hold peeps accountable based on agreed upon core values."

"Your cracks have moved to clarity," Rubystar responded in a voice that evoked the *knowing*.

The gravel crunched until the wheels slid onto the smooth road. The descent back to Hornstown felt like a moment of clarity. As they cruised, Peter used the time to dictate the outline of his plan to Rubystar.

With the revelatory night embedded into his soul and spirit, Peter slept until high noon. The last thought that canvassed his mind was a clip of Coach G's effervescent smile from his introductory video years ago in Uville.

The next day dawned. The grass seemed greener, the sky clearer, and his world sharper. Vision had brought a newfound clarity. To Peter's delight, Rubystar's email was at the top of his inbox. He opened the file to reveal his growth plan – refined, polished, and ready to shine.

20/20 Vision Growth Action Plan

✓ *Create a Compelling Leadership Platform with my team*

✓ *Meet with direct report GM team and whiteboard "phrase that pays" ideas*

✓ *Identify three focus areas to support the vision*

✓ *Name consistent language across the market (support three areas of focus)*

✓ *Visual representation of Visionary Leadership Platform for all team members*

Invest in Others and Grow Leadership

1. *Lead a monthly leadership development training for all entry-level managers.*

2. *Monthly team events for GM, entry-level leaders, and high-potential team members*

3. *Accountability for New Team Member Onboarding Processes*

Monday ushered in a renewed swagger. The glow on his face reflected off his team members' faces as he strutted to his office door. He penned out the agenda for Friday's meeting:

Next-Level Visionary Leadership

The buzz of excitement rippled through his team in anticipation of the meeting. Peter delivered the goods and the team valued the process of working hand-in-hand to create clarity of vision. They struggled to align on a common language that pinpointed their key focus areas, but once they did, they celebrated the idea of coming together to solve their issues. A greater purpose –

something bigger than themselves – had come forth, something they could all believe in.

Their *"Phrase that Pays"* – their core motivator – was simply:

Grow Together!

They developed clear focus headers to support the mission:

Grow Community, Grow Team Members, Grow the Business

They created a framework of unified actions to support each focus item for all to follow. Weekly accountability touchpoints were arranged to coach through the process.

Focus, Communication, and *Fun* were their value torch to light the platform.

The plan was lit. It was time to spotlight it to all 400 team members. They crafted a powerful visual image that expressed the vision... and all general managers committed to being their gym's clock tower... heralding the message.

Peter embraced the gatekeeper role. He set reminders and notifications to shift his leadership mindset. Each club visit, each conference call, and each one-on-one manager touch point focused on narrow communication on the goals of the unified vision.

It didn't take long for his buzzwords to take root in the team's mindset. Once the mindset shifted, Peter could see the next level of engagement in their actions. It was another reminder for his *"Knowing and Growing"* expanding truths that mindset changes behavior. The language became unified, values elevated, and much to his elation, peer-to-peer positive pressure improved the execution of their focus items.

Peter's crown jewel of fulfillment was the transformation of entry-level managers. Over the coming months, his investment in their leadership development expedited the market's performance. The training connected them to next-level leadership as his General Managers created individual growth development plans for their advancement.

That was the jackpot.

The managerial roles stabilized. Their created focus items for rebuilding a unified framework for onboarding entry-level team members were electric. The collective team's synergy skyrocketed with the new monthly team events. The community vibe blew up with solid inter-team relationships.

The results were born again. Market leadership roles were always filled with new leaders waiting in the wings. Turnover decreased; engagement elevated. The vision of *Grow Together*! transformed the market culture.

Peter highlighted the market's momentum with unwavering clarity. The following year, another winning ticket. Despite rising competition, his FitLife team distinguished themselves by their commitment to career development. Leadership growth, team culture, and talent development became the foundational pillars that set them apart.

Peter found his focus.

MY GROWTHTIME!

COACH Q

Deep breath... this is the finisher! The hardest part. Are you ready? Time to master the final fundamental growth zone of being a great 21st-century leader. The finish line is calling your name.

Here are the facts:

The cry of the Gen Z and Millennial workforce howls through the workplace. 75% say that an organization's community engagement and societal impact are important in their work. A recent Harris Poll showed that 76% view business as a source of powerful and positive social impact. They are looking for a specific mission and vision statement to connect with.

Fidelity reported they are willing to take a $7600 pay cut to work for a company with a better team culture.[5]

A Gallup poll showed that worldwide, 80% need to be more engaged or were actively disengaged with their job. Only about half of Gen Zs (51%) and Millennials (56%) rate their mental health as good or extremely good.[6]

The answer is found in you. You are the solution. When you buck the trend and lead with mission, vision, and values... people will gravitate toward you. It is what you want. It is what you must create. It is the clear path to navigate change.

The most powerful force is vision. Even God spoke light into the darkness and established vision at creation. Creating a leadership platform is pure titanium for your team, family, and workplace.

Allowing their input into creating that team vision empowers ownership, engagement, and employee retention... Yes, it even elevates performance.

ASSESSMENT

Two segments below shine a light on visionary leadership. Scaling yourself from 1 –10 will give you a basic performance evaluation. The first segment contains questions for you to answer:

Self:

- I have a clear leadership platform in place for my team [   ]

- I speak daily to our vision (a phrase that pays) [   ]

- I have a unified language with clear focus items for my team [   ]

- I often coach values as a vehicle to hold accountability [   ]

The second is for your team to answer:

Team:

- There is a clear vision inspiring my work [   ]

- My leader speaks daily to our vision [   ]

- There are clear focus items unifying my work [   ]

- Values are often discussed in the workplace as a standard of excellence [   ]

GROWTHTIME

Time to grab that growth journal. I am sure it is close by, or you left it under your pillow. Spend 30 minutes exploring, in detail, the following two questions:

- What is your current vision for your team?

- What "cracks" or "roadblocks" are blurring your vision?

Follow in Peter's footsteps and create your own Leadership Platform:

1. Bring your team together for a whiteboarding session

2. Coach your team on the Leadership Platform *Purpose Plan* (WHY, HOW, WHAT)

3. Align on a clear "phrase that pays"

4. Create three clear focus items with specific actions to unify the language

5. Align the top three Core Values to represent your team

6. Create a fun visual to present your Leadership Platform

Oh wait... one last thing to finish! As a visionary leader, what steps will you take to speak to the vision?

ENCOURAGEMENT

The cracks will mend, and the roadblocks will be removed. Stay true to your messaging and lead with vision, keep accountability with values, and coach to aligned-focused items. You will change the world you influence. Expect a spike in engagement... a jolt of ownership... and the retention of good team members!

Additional resources are available at mygrowthtime.com

CUP OF CHAMPIONS

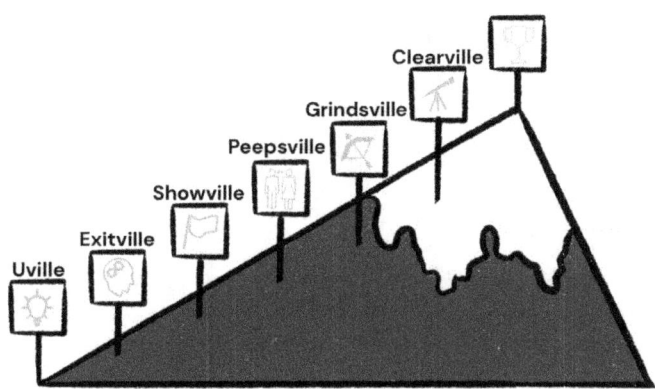

The warm spring breeze blew the aroma of roses across Peter's backyard patio. Inhaling the perfume, he kicked up his feet and reclined in his well-worn rocking chair. He took a refreshing long swig of home sun-brewed sweet tea and closed his eyes as the heartland rays blushed his cheeks.

Almost a year had passed since his Clearville encounter. Life was good. Even with the growing competition, the market held its own. Hornstown's footprint was ready for expansion to leadership's hungry eyes.

The joy of fatherhood saddled Peter's heart. The flow of work-life balance was effortless. Gratitude filled his thoughts as he faded in and out of light snooze, listening to his soulful shuffle. He could hear the sweet jingle of a message from RubyStar: "I've seen fire, and I've seen rain. I've seen sunny days that I thought would never end... I've seen lonely times when I could not find a friend."[7]

Life was funny. Life was messy. Life delivered unique seasons. Despite the fiery trials and rainy seasons, he wouldn't have changed a thing. The voice of growth worked for his good. His future was bright; he just wondered how it would unfold. But before any hopes or ideas could be conceived, the well-known *ping* sent him scrabbling for his phone.

It read:

> *Congrats, you have finished Course #6, The Power of 20/20 Vision! It is time to celebrate you as a new MPA graduate. Congrats on unlocking your best life & leadership. I am proud to stand for you. I will reach out with details but start firing up your graduation speech.*
>
> *Absolutely amazing.*
>
> *Mad love and respect,*
> *Coach G*

Peter shot up and launched into orbit. His head kissed the moon before he floated down. Marvelous, indescribable fulfillment pulsed through his body. His thirst was quenched as he drank the sweet taste of triumph from the legendary Cup of Champions.

With shoulders back and chest high, Peter dashed through the back door to announce the powerful news. The celebration popped out of the bottle as unparalleled harmony filled the house. The completion confirmed what he knew: The future was locked in. Nothing would be impossible to overcome.

Peter had mastered the foundational fundamentals of life and leadership. The clear path was revealed, and a world of possibilities unlocked. The news spread like wildfire. Jhonny's post on the MPA thread created a blaze of congratulatory chimes:

Congrats!

So proud of you,

The legend grows.

Your legacy is unshakeable.

The chocolate icing on the cake was Coach G's call. The voice of a proud coach poured sugar on his heart. Peter thanked Coach G for helping him carry his cross through the rugged terrain when the fatigue wall seemed unsurmountable.

It was the day of all days.

The details of graduation arrived on Sunday, accompanied by a large package from MPA headquarters. Peter dashed for the kitchen with the euphoria of a kid on Christmas morning. His steak knife razored through the tightly sealed box before he carefully unwrapped the thick layers of bubble wrap.

Peter unraveled an engraved trophy as a moon crescent smile touched his ears.

He bearhugged the shiny hardware, savoring the moment of personal triumph. The trophy would find a proud spot beside his bedside table, a constant reminder of his achievement for years to come.

Peter beat the sunrise the next day and bolted to his desk. He stripped the wood off his pencil and crafted out his keynote speech outline. Public speaking was uncharted territory – a fresh road that rekindled the fluttering butterflies he hadn't felt since his pre-game basketball days. He scribed pages filled with stories, testimonies, and lessons to share with his MPA peers. The thought of condensing his ascending journey into a thirty-minute speech felt like a daunting challenge.

By lunchtime, the dust settled, opening up a clear path to narrow his speech. He dove into the Google portal, uncovering a wealth of valuable resources to help him structure his message. MPA even sent over an invaluable one-page overview on the art of public speaking. The true challenge, however, lay in the details: slowing his delivery, maintaining steady eye contact with the camera, infusing humor, and, most importantly, speaking from the heart. It was a delicate balance, but one that would make all the difference.

Peter took practice shots, recording and reviewing his speech, as the clock sprinted towards graduation day. One more tick... and the dial struck the hour.

He took a deep breath, brushed aside his hair, and settled into his white leather office chair. His knees locked in under his elevated desk. His palms were dry, and his hands were steady. Butterflies a distant memory as the arena readied to open. In a flash, the thought appeared... could speaking be his next adventure? The thought didn't have a splash to anchor as the window opened.

Coach G took the virtual stage, his presence larger than life, and welcomed the hundreds of friends, family and fellow MPAs who had jumped on to his elated surprise. Peter unleashed a grin in thankfulness. Trevor, Arian, Rochelle, Mr. Mustang, and countless others tuned in, adding to the growing crowd. Coach G began, "Thank you for coming out today to celebrate Peter, a beloved and devoted MPA who has overcome life's adversity to fulfill his noble quest to graduate from the academy. We all know *Max-Potential Academy* is not for the faint of heart or the weak of mind. It takes work to unlock your best life & leadership. *GrowthTime!* is never easy. It requires massive courage to master the fundamental lessons.

"The road is winding, filled with storms, roadblocks, and curveballs on the way to reaching your potential and becoming a great 21st-century leader. Congrats on enduring with an excellent spirit. I am proud and honored to introduce our graduate... Peter!"

Peter fought to hold back the tears welling in his eyes as the thunderous applause gradually faded into silence. The words dropped, "Well, I am overwhelmed, stuck in awe, with seeing all of you show up today." Peter paused with one last internal gathering. "Looks like you all graduated, Showville," Peter said with a half-cocked glimmer to roaring laughter.

"Before I share my growth journey, I would like to thank Coach G, Jhonny, and the support of my MPA Community. Without you, I wouldn't be here. Thank you for believing in me before I believed in myself. Thank you, Jhonny, for reaching out to that broken, mask-wearing kid all those years ago in the Bluffs. Coach G, you are beyond good. However, I recommend we change the good for growth," Peter shouted to the agreeing audience who cheered, bringing a glorious mist to Coach G's eyes. "You are the best *Growth Coach* in the business!"

Peter's voice trembled, heart fluttering as he said, "Thank you for being my Growth Coach – for your unwavering care, steadfast commitment, and proving your trustworthiness. Your guidance has truly been transformative. I only hope I can change the world like you have changed mine."

Peter took a deliberate pause and gathered himself before shifting gears.

"Life is messy," he said. "Leadership is humbling. Villains, robbers and bad characters are part of any story. The good news is the voice of growth is greater than all. The voice is an overcoming sound that must be heard. Today, I am going to share lessons learned with high hopes that they will inspire your journey. I am confident the voice of growth will speak tonight, so be ready. These lessons have been branded into my flesh and worked to purify my soul."

For the next 25 minutes, Peter exuded unwavering confidence, commanding the room with his passion. He surprised even himself with each antidotal transformation story shared about each location. The audience was fully captivated – laughing, tearing up, and erupting into cheers as his words brought the journeys to life.

Peter took the last few moments to highlight the powerful growth lessons that had benchmarked his journey:

The Lessons of My Life and Leadership Journey

Uville – The Power of U!

- I am Humanity + Divinity: There is a *Purpose Plan* for my life
- Daily death-to-self breaks the Pride-Ego and allows for my growth

Exitville – The Power of Beliefs

- Our limiting or empowering beliefs are the battleground for our future
- Choose faith, self-declarations, and dependent-trust to overcome Exitville

Showville – The Power of Personal Liberty

- Knowledge is key: Body, Soul & Spirit
- Personal freedom allows you to overcome the hypocrite monster

Peepsville – Power to the People

- Ownership & Empowerment are foundational principles of leadership
- Savage conversations are the catalyst for change

Grindsville – The Power of Performance

- Grow the Wheel of Performance: people, process, productivity
- Coach Leaders are motivated by relationships leading to growth

Clearville – The Power of 20/20 Vision

- A clear Leadership Platform will unify your team
- Lead with vision to lead through change

Peter was consumed by fire. An inward blaze as his words torched forth – a powerful purpose as he commanded the airwaves. "Reaching and living to our potential requires us to stop in each of these locations. There is a season and purpose for each one. Each one presented power – the power of choice." He paused. "The power to choose growth or stagnation. To choose hope or hopelessness. To choose life or death."

Peter continued with a soul-Southern Baptist preacher voice, "I now feel confident, secure, and empowered to navigate the enemies that war against my story. No matter how tough it is, how painful your journey has become, or what villain you are facing, keep pressing through. More love, more joy, and a powerful testimony of character are budding in your life. Get ready to shine!"

With each slow, steady beat of his heart, Peter's confidence grew. Grounding the moment, he declared, "Your leadership... your leadership will blossom with greater authority, game-changing results, and a vision that your peeps will run through walls to achieve. *You are strong in life and leadership*."

Opening his hands, he said, "This is what Coach G calls the *Growthlife* – more *love, joy, character, authority, results,* and *vision* – the fruit of all your growth. Nothing will be impossible! Thank you! And it's always *GrowthTime!*"

Coach G stared into Peter's eyes, releasing a glow of pride as the words struck gold. After an eternal loop of cheering, Coach G settled the audience, "Well, you dropped the mic, Peter. The speaking circuit should take notice. Congrats again, and we are thankful to have an amazing MPA representative like you leading the charge. In honor of your achievement, your name will be inscribed on the MPA wall of fame. Keep up the growth work! Thank you, everyone, for coming. Make it a wonderful growth life."

As Coach G stood up, Peter noticed a name badge embroidered over the coach's heart. It was one word:

It was a glorious day.

COACH Q – THE LAST WORD

What a ride! I am confident you held on tight with Peter on his *GrowthTime!* journey. The path is clear, the roadmap secure, and powerful guidance is available to you... leading your quest to claim the trophy of your best life and stepping into the 21st-century leader God created you to be.

Life is a contact sport. You are going to go through trials, hardships, financial pain, relationship struggles, and break ups. It's all kinds of drama. Your best life isn't a life of financial security, the American dream, and living on a beach sipping margaritas.

Your best life is today. Your best life comes from living your *Purpose Plan*, operating through an empowering belief system, and growing a personal liberty that NOTHING will hold you down!

It is time to change the world you influence.

You don't have to be a superstar influencer, have a million followers, or be a successful business leader. Changing the world starts with personal growth. It starts with changing the world in front of you today.

Nothing more, nothing less.

One person. One event. One interaction.

Be a world–changer! Our culture is in desperate need of leaders like you. And now... I am curious as to how you feel? How did you get on with this journey? Did you pause and jump into your *GrowthTime!* or just read the book straight through?

My guess is curiosity kept you reading, but now is the time to heed the voice of growth. Yes, Coach says go back to Uville's *GrowthTime!* and put in the growth work. Don't cheat yourself or others who are depending on you.

They need you to show up *strong* in *Life* and *Leadership!*

I know it isn't easy. If it were... the world would be filled with MPA graduates. Every problem would be solved, the world would flow in harmony, and nothing would be impossible. Just commit to taking the first step. The hardest step is the first step. I am cheering for you. Coach G is shouting your name.

GrowthTime! has been growing in me for over 20 years. Amazingly, this narrative story is autobiographical, based on true events for movie lovers, and recalls my personal growth journey to unlock my best life & leadership.

My story started almost an eternity ago after I graduated from Davidson College in 1996. Much to my disappointment, I went undrafted in the NBA out of college. If the record early entry draft class of Kobe Bryant, Allen Iverson, and Ray Allen had only stayed in school!

Ironically, the Omaha Racers drafted me in the first round of the now-defunct NBA feeder league, the Continental Basketball Association (CBA). In the brutal cold of my life in the winter of 1997, my world was revolutionized. I was introduced to the Great Growth Coach – The Lord Himself – through a dear friend and teammate, Ronni Grandison. Coach God lifted me out of my distorted Uville, breathing new life into my hardened heart and awakening a passion to transform the lost, dying world around me.

Within months, I was captivated by the voice of growth.

With Coach speaking confidence into my soul, I leapfrogged from the end of the bench to playoff starter, grew into a top 20 minor league prospect, and soon signed a contract with the Los Angeles Clippers.

The *GrowthTime!* storyline followed as I suffered one injury after another for several years in pursuing the dream. The last was multiple herniated disk degeneration in my lower back that progressed to leaving me incapacitated over a two-year battle... despite care from elite doctors.

Set for major back surgery at the age of 26, the Divine intervened. In truth, if you can believe, if it were not for a miraculous touch from Jesus on July 1st, 2001, at 9p.m., I would have stayed a physical wreck, unable to operate in life.

God is Gooood!

I was completely healed in an instant at a church service in Las Vegas, of all places. Over 20 years later, no surgery and never an ounce of back pain.

During this period of adversity, I identified with the lessons of Exitville and wrestled with the power of beliefs. I could have gone back to self-reliance and self-doubt, but Coach kept moving my mindset and faith forward. I learned the power of choice and reaped internal joy during the raging storm.

Healed, with a newborn son in tow, I took a flyer doing sales with the fitness industry giant 24-Hour Fitness. It was a wild, crazy, fun ride filled with mountaintop and valley-low memories. During my career, I grew from Sales Leader to Sales Manager, General Manager, and Area Manager.

I will forever love the passion of my fitness peeps and the impact fitness makes on one's life.

And yes, unfortunately, the personal crisis was real. Navigating the relationship breakup was gut-wrenching. From a family breakup to a failed business partner start-up, leaving 24Hour Fitness, and seasons of financial barrenness... all the while embracing and growing in understanding the *Power of Personal Liberty*. Learning to rise above and show up despite my circumstances was necessary growth!

During my second stint with 24Hour Fitness, I discovered a deep passion for leadership. Transitioning from Peepsville to Clearville, I became determined to relentlessly pursue my potential as a leader. Leadership was the end goal and not just the means to the end.

As my tree sprouted within 24Hour Fitness, I focused on one simple goal: changing the world within my influence. Fulfillment filled my soul as I turned my personal growth lessons into tools to empower the growth of others. I found significance!

The COVID world created the opportunity for *GrowthTime!* to move from experience to paper. With 24Hour Fitness in a well-publicized financial crisis, change was hurtling my way. My job was eliminated, and almost two decades of service came to a close. It was time to "pivot" with the rest of the world.

How could I change the world I influence? The vision came in the late summer of 2020 after reflecting, coaching and prayer. I penned out the fundamental "growth zones" one night until 3 in the morning. Each growth zone is represented by the towns in the story. The growth zones led to the creation of the *GrowthTime!* coaching platform – drawing on painful lessons of growth to streamline the process for the next generation.

And...

I began to coach! Client after client proved the power of these lessons and their transformative power.

You see the reality clearly – it's undeniable and in plain view. Our culture is crying out in profound pain. We need value-driven coach leaders motivated by relationships to grow their peeps' *lives* and *leadership*.

Your people carry their problems, stress, and anxiety into the workplace every day – diminishing productivity and weakening performance. They need you, Coach, to step up with powerful guidance and tools to drive their growth and development. You are the solution. You are the answer.

GrowthTime! is the vehicle to power their journey from darkness into the light.

It is the ultimate path to change the world within your influence.

Strengthen your mind. Stabilize your foundation. An energized, fulfilled, purpose-driven life is within your grasp. It is just ahead. You will make an impact on the generation you serve. You will overcome yourself and crush limiting beliefs that threaten your mission. You will provide guidance, accountability, and support to those you love and lead.

You will be an MPA graduate!

COACH'S CHALLENGE

3 Steps of Action

1. ***Get Connected***

   Go to mygrowthtime.com and receive free weekly mindset coaching by signing up for Monday Movers Mindset.

2. **Start Your Journey**

   Go to mygrowthtime.com and start the unique newsletter course, a 48-week *GrowthTime!* journey through all six growth zones (all for less than renting an Amazon Prime movie each month).

3. **Go Deep**

   Visit mygrowthtime.com and sign up for the intensive, exclusive online coaching course: *The Power of U!*

Lastly...

☺ If *GrowthTime!* has inspired or changed your life, pay it forward! Send a copy to that person you are thinking of right now.

It is your time for GrowthTime!

> *May God, the Great Growth Coach, powerfully move you forward on your mission. God, give them clarity of vision on their way, show them breakthrough truths, and empower them to move into life-changing action. Coach them to fulfill their maximum potential in life, leadership, and business. Bless the work of their hands and the fruit of their lips. Power amazing results! In Jesus' name.*

> *God's best is always ahead,*

> *Coach Q*

ACKNOWLEDGMENTS

I am deeply and speechlessly grateful for the unwavering love and support of my mom, Joanne Harwood, whose wisdom and prayers have been the spiritual backbone of my journey in writing *GrowthTime!* Your encouragement has been a constant strength.

To the loving memory of my father, Terry Harwood, whose belief in this vision and blessing over the work of my hands gave me the confidence to pursue this mission. Your legacy of "Help Others, Help Others" lives on in these pages.

To the next generation, my children Jacob, Christian & Grace – may you change the world you influence as your lives have forever changed mine.

And above all, to Jesus, the author and finisher of my story, who held my heart through every doubt and guided my pen through every word. Thank you for being the source of my strength, the inspiration behind the words, and the grace that brought this to life.

ENDNOTES

1   Eminem (2002). *Lose Yourself*. Detroit, Michigan: Eminem. Available at: https://www.youtube.com/watch?v=_Yhyp-_hX2s [Accessed 20 Nov. 2024].

2   American Pie. (2017). *Don McLean*. Available at: https://www.youtube.com/watch?v=iX_TFkut1PM.

3   Retrospective Soundtrack. 2016. "Steppenwolf – Born to Be Wild (Easy Rider) (1969)." YouTube Video. *YouTube*. https://www.youtube.com/watch?v=egMWlD3fLJ8.

4   Garvin, D. (2013). *How Google Sold Its Engineers on Management*. [online] Harvard Business Review. Available at: https://hbr.org/2013/12/how-google-sold-its-engineers-on-management.

5   Evaluate a Job Offer Study. (n.d.). Available at: https://www.fidelity.com/bin-public/060_www_fidelity_com/documents/fidelity-job-offer-fact-sheet.pdf.

6   Deloitte (2024). *The Deloitte Global 2024 Gen Z and Millennial Survey*. [online] Deloitte. Available at: https://www.deloitte.com/global/en/issues/work/content/genz-millennialsurvey.html.

7   "James Taylor – Fire and Rain (Official Audio)." n.d. www.youtube.com. https://www.youtube.com/watch?v=EbD7lfrsY2s.